THE ART OF
Spaghetti Cookery

BY MYRA WALDO

THE ART OF SPAGHETTI COOKERY

THE ART OF SOUTH AMERICAN COOKERY

COOKING FOR THE FREEZER

BEER AND GOOD FOOD

1001 WAYS TO PLEASE A HUSBAND

DINING OUT IN ANY LANGUAGE

TRAVEL GUIDE TO EUROPE

THE COMPLETE ROUND-THE-WORLD COOKBOOK

CO-AUTHOR

THE MOLLY GOLDBERG JEWISH COOKBOOK
With Gertrude Berg

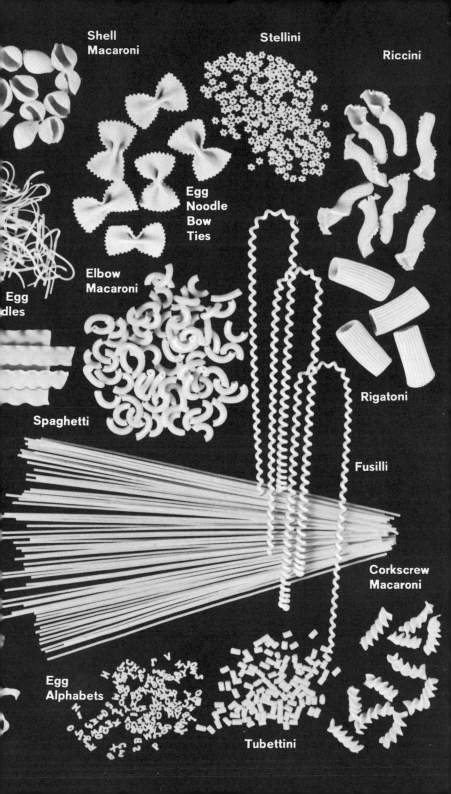

THE ART OF
Spaghetti Cookery

by

MYRA WALDO

GARDEN CITY, NEW YORK

Doubleday & Company, Inc.

1964

Contents

Introduction

THE smallest American town has its Italian restaurant, for Italian food is particularly appealing to our taste. Of all Italian dishes, nothing can match spaghetti in popularity, and Americans seem to enjoy a plate of spaghetti more than almost any other food. Spaghetti dishes are not just Italian, however, as almost every country includes them in its cuisine.

While spaghetti may have become popular in the United States only within recent memory, it has been a favorite in other parts of the world for thousands of years. It is usually assumed that spaghetti—and in fact the whole family of macaroni—is inherited from Italy and that the Italians originated it. This belief is readily understood, for the Italians have developed a seemingly endless array of recipes based upon this most delicious food.

At the risk of destroying a favorite myth, it seems unlikely that Italy was the first country to produce those "strands of paste" which we call spaghetti. The earliest records of dough formed into a standardized shape and boiled in water go back a very long way, to almost 3000 B.C. One of the earliest cookbooks in existence is the *Hon-Zo*, a Chinese text which contains cookery instructions for that period, including one for a type of cooked dough very much like present-day spaghetti. Even older than the *Hon-Zo* are several Japanese cookbooks (dating back to approximately 3500 B.C.) which also describe cooked-dough dishes, although these call for rice-flour noodles rather than wheat. In addition to using wheat (as in our modern product), the Chinese method seems closer to the modern version of spaghetti, and therefore it seems likely that spaghetti as we know it today originated in China. This is not to refute the story that spaghetti may have actually been an Italian innovation, completely without the knowledge of the Chinese, and it may well be that this delicious preparation began independently in both China and Italy, at completely separate times in history.

There are several favorite rumors that should be discussed, chiefly the one about that great traveler and explorer, Marco Polo, who lived from about 1254 to 1323. Marco was a remarkable man and during his lifetime accomplished many notable achievements, but he has been incorrectly credited with bringing spaghetti from China. It is an attractive, easily believed story, but the weight of evidence is against him. When Marco was a rather young man, his father and uncle, both traders, took him overland on a trading trip into China. What may now be accomplished in a matter of hours in a jet plane took several long, tedious years on foot until the strongly knit Italian family reached the Chinese court. The Chinese emperor took a fancy to Marco, and he remained there for many years, holding important court positions. It is said that, while in China, Marco saw the spaghetti-making process and when he returned home to Venice showed his fellow Italians how to make the delicious strings.

Fables, however, have a way of playing false, no matter how enjoyable they may be in the telling. The fact is that *pasta* (then generally called macaroni) was well known in Italy for several centuries before Marco's lifetime. But written evidence is the best, and there is still in existence a religious book written in Italy and published in A.D. 1200 (more than a half century before Marco was born) called *The Life of the Blessed Hermit William*. In this long tale of the religious life of a hermit the following sentence appears: "He invited William to dinner and served macaroni." It is therefore obvious that macaroni was known in Italy before Marco's birth. To carry the evidence one step farther, in Marco's book describing his adventures (written upon his return to Venice), he mentions seeing the Chinese cooks make large pieces of dough, which he refers to as *lasagne*—a fact that indicates he undoubtedly had seen and eaten *lasagne* at home in Venice before his trip to China.

Another folk tale concerns itself with how macaroni got its name. The legend would have one believe that there was a noted chef named Cico who worked for a prince who had an appreciation of new dishes. The chef prepared a new creation of dough and served it to his royal master, who immediately exclaimed, "*Oh, ma caroni!*" which may be roughly translated as "Oh, how very dear!" It is an amusing story, but it is no more likely to be true than the one about Marco Polo.

The fact is that spaghetti was, and is, an enormously popular dish because both China and Italy needed a tasty dish that was not only filling but also cheap. In Italy, wheat grows readily, but there is comparatively little land suitable for cattle grazing, and therefore the cuisine of the country turned toward a basic starchy food. Perhaps this is an appropriate time to clear up the difference between macaroni and spaghetti, if indeed there is a valid distinction. *Macaroni* is a general term used to embrace all the various types of doughs cooked in a wide variety of shapes. For those who are unacquainted with the world of *pasta*, it should be mentioned that in Italy (and in Italian food shops in the United States) there are in the neighborhood of one hundred different types of *pasta*, the Italian word for all of the pastes, or boiled doughs, used in the Italian cuisine. A visit to an Italian food shop reveals that *pasta* comes not only in the usual shape that Americans know and call spaghetti, a medium-sized type, but also in an amazing, almost bewildering assortment of lengths, shapes, and sizes. There is the very thin, almost hairlike *capelli d'angelo*, or angel's hair; there are progressively larger ones until spaghetti is reached, representing a sort of halfway mark in the gradation of sizes. Then there are larger types such as *mezzani*, so large that merely one, stuffed with a filling, makes a portion. Some *pasta* are solid, whereas others are hollow; one type presents a smooth surface, another is ridged; and so it goes, apparently in endless variety, limited only by the imagination of the maker. Fancy shapes are usual, too—needles, turbans, hats, sea shells, rooster's crests, butterflies, and rings, to mention just a few. The Italians give their *pasta* familiar pet names, as for example *stellini* (little stars) and *mostaccioli* (little mustaches).

To return to spaghetti, the Italian word for string is *spago*, and spaghetti is therefore merely "little strings."

Many Anglo-Saxons, familiar only with spaghetti and macaroni, often question the need for so many different sizes and shapes of *pasta*. Don't they all taste alike? Don't they all serve the same purpose, covered with a sauce? Most efforts to explain the purpose of the wide variety of *pasta* shapes and forms are likely to be unsuccessful, for words fail, whereas taste does not. The only way to explain why a certain type of *pasta* is particularly suitable with a clam sauce, for instance, is to taste the dish prepared with two different types of *pasta*. For centuries the Italians have served *linguini* with clam sauce, finding this flat type best with the succulent shellfish. Why a flat *pasta* provides a more suitable combination with a clam sauce than a rounded type does (like spaghetti, for example) is somewhat difficult to explain, but the fact remains that generations of Italians must be right. But this is merely one example. The chefs in Bologna in northern Italy would rather not serve a *pasta* with a rich meat sauce if that *pasta* were not the delectable flat noodles of dough called *pappardelle*. Then, too, there are the various types of *pasta* in fancy hollow forms, many of which can be stuffed; when one eats *cavatelle*, those little sea shells of dough, the filling squeezes out delightfully, offering an entirely different taste sensation from that experienced while eating a long type of *pasta*. The gastronomically curious are urged to try as many different types of *pasta* as possible.

Macaroni and its associated types became popular several centuries ago in Europe. Throughout western Europe it was considered extremely chic to serve macaroni, and it had the same connotation among the cognoscenti then as caviar and *pâté de foie gras* have at the present time. By the end of the eighteenth century the Italian word *macaroni* crept into the English language, but with two meanings. The first was the true meaning with reference to the food itself, the second that of a dandy or fop, a man who traveled abroad and wore elaborate, dandified clothes, for at that time the eating of macaroni was associated in the public mind with persons of that type. Both meanings traveled to the United States, for as the famous song goes:

Yankee Doodle came to town
Riding on a pony
He stuck a feather in his cap
And called it macaroni.

The Americans liked macaroni from Revolutionary days on, but it was only moderately popular at first, for meat, fish, and poultry were plentiful and very reasonably priced. That extraordinary American, Thomas Jefferson, an unusually ingenious and inventive man, spent considerable time and effort in Italy searching for a spaghetti-making machine. From early colonial times *pasta* has been made in the United States, but the quantities were modest and the public acceptance never great. With the coming of Prohibition during the twenties, Americans turned to speakeasies and restaurants where liquor was available. Among the most popular places were the Italian restaurants, serving Chianti and other red wines. The American public developed a great liking for spaghetti, and from that time on, public demand soared. Having enjoyed spaghetti in a restaurant, people began to serve it at home. Domestic production increased, and at the same time imports from abroad grew to substantial volume. American production know-how met the demand, and soon spaghetti and its allied products became an important American food industry. It is said that more spaghetti is sold in New York City than in any other city in the world.

Originally, during its earliest days in Italy, macaroni was made by mixing flour and water, rolling it flat, cutting it into desired shapes and lengths, and then drying it in the open air. Today more modern, sanitary methods are employed. As in the early days, only a special type of wheat, called durum, known for its hardness, is used. It has a high gluten content with low starch; the ordinary soft type of wheat used in making bread would be too soft for spaghetti and would result in a soggy finished product. When the durum wheat is ground into a coarse meal, with the bran content removed, it is called semolina. Some experimental spaghetti and noodles have been made with other substances, such as soybeans, artichokes, and rice, but their popularity and acceptance by the public has never been great. Incidentally, noodles are somewhat allied to *pasta*, except that they contain approximately 5 per cent egg yolk solids by law. At the present time noodles make up about 15 per cent of the total market for macaroni and allied products. The word "noodle" itself is not of Italian origin and undoubtedly comes from the German *nudel*; the Germans are considered noodle-eaters in a class by themselves.

Finally, a note of good cheer. Most people think spaghetti and other types of *pasta* are wildly fattening. They aren't. A 4-ounce serving of most *pasta* averages about 105 calories; even 4 ounces of roast chicken has 210. It is true that the sauce on your spaghetti adds some calories, but all in all, a plate of spaghetti isn't any more fattening than almost any other food.

MYRA WALDO

How to Cook Perfect Spaghetti Every Time

FIRST, be sure your spaghetti (or other *pasta*) is fresh; if it remains on your shelf too long, it may lose flavor. Next, cook it as close to serving time as possible. Be sure to use a very large pot, one of at least 8 quarts capacity.

Fill the pot with fresh, *cold* water; never use hot. Add 2 tablespoons of salt and bring to a violent, rolling boil; that is, the surface of the water should be moving vigorously and steadily. Add 1 pound of whatever *pasta* you are cooking, but don't break the strands, even if they are fairly long. Instead, wait a minute, then nudge them gently into the pot with a fork after the portion in the boiling water has softened. If you like a very smooth *pasta* and one that will not stick to the sides of the pot, add 1 teaspoon of butter or olive oil. Stir the *pasta* once in a while, preferably with a large wooden spoon.

Don't overcook! Italians feel that most Americans eat their spaghetti far too well cooked. They ought to know, and they prefer it *al dente*, literally "to the tooth," which means that the cooked *pasta* offers the very slightest degree of resistance to the tooth when eaten. Read the instructions on the package of *pasta* and then, just about 3 or 4 minutes before the suggested time, begin to taste a strand or two. The instructions usually allow too much time, and the spaghetti will taste better when cooked slightly under the specified time. With a little experimentation you can determine the ideal cooking time for a particular brand of *pasta*. In any event, the degree of doneness is a matter of individual taste. When the spaghetti is cooked to your personal satisfaction, remove the pot from the heat and immediately add a cup of cold water. This stops the cooking action, which would otherwise continue (although somewhat more slowly) even though removed from the heat. Do not rinse the *pasta* under cold water, or it will become cold. Turn the *pasta* into a large colander, shake until all the water is drained, and then you're ready for one of the tastiest foods encountered by man.

With Cheese

*P*ASTA with Parmesan cheese is a classic, but there are many other cheeses that enhance the flavor of the dish. Combinations of cheeses are particularly good, each blending with the other, to create a new flavor. Serve one of the recipes in this section as a main course, as a welcome change from the usual meat, poultry, or fish. For best results, always use freshly grated cheese. It takes just a few extra seconds, and the difference will be well worth the effort.

CHEESE-NOODLE PIE

(Noodle Beoreg)

½ pound cottage cheese
½ pound cream cheese
2 cups (½ pound) grated cheddar cheese
1 teaspoon salt
¼ teaspoon pepper

3 eggs, beaten
¼ cup chopped dill or parsley
1 pound broad noodles, cooked and drained
4 tablespoons butter

Beat the cottage cheese and cream cheese together until smooth. Beat in the cheddar cheese, salt, pepper, and eggs. Divide the mixture in half, and add the dill or parsley to one half.

Butter an oblong baking dish. Spread half the noodles in it. Cover with cheese, dill or parsley mixture, then remaining noodles. Spread the cheese mixture on top. Dot with the butter. Bake in a

350° oven 25 minutes, or until delicately browned. Cut into squares and serve hot.

Serves 4–6.

BAKED LASAGNE WITH THREE CHEESES
(Lasagne al Forno ai Tre Formaggi)

3 tablespoons olive oil
1 cup minced onions
1 cup thinly sliced green peppers
2 cloves garlic, minced
1½ teaspoons salt
¼ teaspoon pepper
½ teaspoon orégano
2 tablespoons chopped parsley
1 29-ounce can tomatoes
1 8-ounce can tomato sauce
½ cup grated dry Gouda or Edam cheese
½ pound lasagne (1½-inch wide noodles)
¾ pound sliced Swiss cheese
1½ pounds cottage cheese

Heat the olive oil; sauté the onions, green peppers, and garlic 10 minutes. Add the salt, pepper, orégano, parsley, tomatoes, and tomato sauce. Cover and cook over low heat 30 minutes. Stir in 2 tablespoons Gouda cheese.

Cook the *lasagne* (if not available, use broad noodles) as package directs. Spread a third of the sauce in a 12-by-8-inch baking dish. Arrange alternate layers of the *lasagne*, Swiss cheese, cottage cheese, a sprinkling of the Gouda, and some of the sauce; repeat until all the ingredients are used up. Cover with the remaining sauce and sprinkle top with remaining Gouda cheese.

Bake in a 350° oven 35 minutes. Serve hot.

Serves 8.

MACARONI WITH THREE CHEESES

(Pasta ai Tre Formaggi)

1 pound macaroni
3 tablespoons butter
1 cup grated Parmesan
cheese

½ cup grated Gruyère or
Swiss cheese
½ cup grated Fontina or
mozzarella cheese
1 cup heavy cream

Use any shape of macaroni you like. Cook in deep, boiling, salted water until tender but still firm. Drain, rinse under cold water, and drain again.

In a casserole, toss the macaroni with the butter, then the three cheeses. Add the cream. Bake in a 400° oven 20 minutes, or until browned.

Serves 4–6.

MACARONI WITH RICOTTA

(Maccheroni con la Ricotta)

½ pound ricotta or cottage
cheese
¾ teaspoon salt
¼ teaspoon freshly ground
black pepper

⅛ teaspoon nutmeg
3 tablespoons hot water
1 pound macaroni, cooked
and drained
Grated Parmesan cheese

In a bowl, mix together the ricotta, salt, pepper, and nutmeg. Beat in the hot water. Toss with the hot macaroni and serve with grated Parmesan cheese.

Serves 4–6.

MACARONI WITH CHEESE AND BACON SAUCE

½ *pound bacon*
1 *pound macaroni, cooked*
  and drained

1 *pound pot cheese or*
  cottage cheese
1½ *cups sour cream*

Fry the bacon until crisp. Drain, reserving 2 tablespoons of the fat. Crumble the bacon. Combine the fat with the macaroni in a saucepan; toss lightly. Add the cheese and sour cream. Cook over very low heat until very hot.

Place macaroni mixture on a hot platter and sprinkle bacon on top.

Serves 4–6.

OLIVE, CHEESE, AND MACARONI CASSEROLE

2 *tablespoons butter*
2 *tablespoons olive oil*
2 *tablespoons flour*
2 *cups milk*
1 *teaspoon salt*

2 *cups grated American*
  cheese
1 *cup sliced pimiento-*
  stuffed olives
1 *pound elbow macaroni,*
  cooked and drained

Heat the butter and olive oil in a saucepan over low heat. Blend in the flour. Gradually add the milk, stirring constantly to the boiling point. Add the salt and cheese. Cook over low heat 5 minutes, stirring frequently. Add the olives.

Place the macaroni in a buttered casserole; pour the sauce over it. Bake in a 375° oven 15 minutes, or until bubbly hot and delicately browned.

Serves 4–6.

CHEESE AND MACARONI CUSTARD

4 eggs
3 cups milk, scalded
½ pound elbow macaroni,
   cooked and drained
2 cups (½ pound) grated
   cheddar cheese

1½ teaspoons salt
¼ teaspoon pepper
½ teaspoon Worcestershire
   sauce

Beat the eggs in a bowl. Gradually add the milk, stirring constantly. Add the macaroni, cheese, salt, pepper, and Worcestershire sauce.

Pour into a buttered 2-quart baking dish. Place the dish in a pan and add water in the pan to a depth of 4 inches.

Bake in a 350° oven 45 minutes, or until set and lightly browned. *Serves 4–6.*

CHEESE AND SPAGHETTI CUSTARD

6 tablespoons butter
¾ cup chopped onions
¼ pound mushrooms,
   sliced
1 cup fresh bread crumbs
1½ cups milk, scalded
4 eggs, beaten
1½ teaspoons salt

¼ teaspoon freshly ground
   black pepper
⅛ teaspoon nutmeg
½ cup grated Parmesan
   cheese
½ pound spaghetti, broken
   into 1-inch pieces,
   cooked and drained

Melt the butter in a skillet; sauté the onions and mushrooms 5 minutes, stirring frequently. Remove from the heat. Soak the bread crumbs in the milk for 5 minutes. Add to the mushroom mixture. Beat in the eggs, salt, pepper, nutmeg, and cheese.

Spread the spaghetti in a buttered casserole. Pour the mushroom mixture over it. Place casserole in a shallow pan of water. Bake in a 325° oven 30 minutes, or until custard is set. *Serves 4–6.*

NOODLE-CHEESE PUDDING

4 eggs
¾ cup sour cream
1 teaspoon salt
2 cups cottage cheese

1 pound fine noodles,
    cooked and drained
4 tablespoons dry bread
    crumbs
3 tablespoons melted butter

Beat the eggs, sour cream, and salt together. Stir in the cheese and noodles. Turn into a buttered 2-quart baking dish or casserole. Sprinkle with the bread crumbs and butter. Bake in a 375° oven 40 minutes.
Serves 6.

SPAGHETTI CROQUETTES

1 tablespoon butter
1 tablespoon flour
¾ cup milk
¾ cup grated cheddar
    cheese
1 teaspoon salt
¼ teaspoon freshly ground
    black pepper
¼ teaspoon dry mustard

2 eggs
½ pound spaghetti, cooked,
    drained, and chopped
1 teaspoon grated onion
1 tablespoon chopped
    parsley
¾ cup dry bread crumbs
Vegetable oil for deep-fat
    frying

Melt the butter in a saucepan. Blend in the flour until smooth. Gradually add the milk, stirring constantly to the boiling point. Mix in the cheese, salt, pepper, and mustard; cook over low heat 5 minutes. Cool 15 minutes. Beat 1 of the eggs and add to the cheese mixture, mixing thoroughly. Add the spaghetti, onion, and parsley. Taste for seasoning. Chill 1 hour. Shape into 12 croquettes.

Beat the remaining egg. Dip the croquettes into the egg and then into the bread crumbs.

Heat the oil to 375°. Fry the croquettes until lightly browned.

Drain and serve hot as a luncheon dish or as an accompaniment to main courses.

Makes 12.

STUFFED SHELLS

(Conchiglie Ripiene)

1 *pound ricotta cheese or cottage cheese*	1 *egg, beaten*
1 *cup grated Parmesan cheese*	1 *pound* conchiglie, *cooked and drained (see note below)*
½ *teaspoon salt*	½ *cup melted butter*
¼ *teaspoon freshly ground black pepper*	

Beat together the ricotta cheese, 3 tablespoons of the Parmesan cheese, the salt, pepper, and egg. Stuff the *conchiglie* very carefully to avoid breaking the shells. Arrange in a buttered baking dish. Sprinkle with the butter and remaining cheese.

Bake in a 350° oven 20 minutes, or until delicately browned. *Serves 4–6.*

NOTE: *Conchiglie* are little shells of dough. If not available, large tubes of macaroni may be substituted.

BAKED MACARONI LAYERS

2 *tablespoons butter*	½ *teaspoon freshly ground pepper*
1 *cup sliced onions*	
2 *cloves garlic, sliced*	1 *pound macaroni, cooked and drained*
2 *cups peeled, chopped tomatoes*	¾ *pound thinly sliced Swiss cheese*
1 *teaspoon salt*	

Melt the butter in a skillet; add onions, garlic, tomatoes, salt, and pepper. Cook over low heat 15 minutes. Add the macaroni.

Mix well. Place half the mixture in a buttered casserole. Arrange half the cheese over it. Cover with remaining macaroni mixture.

Bake in a preheated 425° oven 10 minutes. Arrange remaining cheese on top, and bake 10 minutes longer.

Serves 4.

BAKED MACARONI AND CHEESE

(Pasta Gratinata)

6 *tablespoons butter*
4 *tablespoons flour*
2 *cups milk*
1 *teaspoon salt*
¼ *teaspoon white pepper*

1 *pound macaroni, cooked*
and drained
1 *cup grated Parmesan*
cheese

Melt 4 tablespoons of the butter in a saucepan; blend in the flour. Add the milk, stirring steadily to the boiling point. Mix in the salt and pepper. Cook over low heat 10 minutes.

In a greased casserole, make as many layers as possible of the macaroni, cheese, and sauce. Dot with the remaining butter. Bake in a 400° oven 20 minutes.

Serves 4–6.

COTTAGE CHEESE NOODLE RING

¼ *pound cream cheese*
½ *pound cottage cheese*
2 *eggs*
1 *teaspoon salt*
½ *pound fine noodles,*
cooked and drained

4 *tablespoons melted*
butter
4 *tablespoons dry bread*
crumbs

Beat together the cream cheese, cottage cheese, eggs, and salt until smooth. Mix in the noodles.

Rub a 9-inch ring mold with a little of the melted butter. Dust with some of the bread crumbs. Pour the mixture into it. Mix the remaining butter and bread crumbs together and sprinkle over the top. Bake in a 375° oven 30 minutes, or until set and lightly browned on top. Run a knife around the edge and carefully unmold.

Serves 4.

CHEESE-NOODLE RING

4 tablespoons butter
4 tablespoons flour
2 cups milk
1½ teaspoons salt
¼ teaspoon freshly ground
    black pepper
½ teaspoon dry mustard

1½ cups grated cheddar
    cheese
2 tablespoons grated
    onions
2 eggs, beaten
½ pound fine noodles,
    cooked and drained

Melt the butter in a saucepan; blend in the flour. Gradually add the milk, stirring constantly to the boiling point. Mix in the salt, pepper, and mustard. Cook over low heat 5 minutes, stirring occasionally. Stir in the cheese until melted. Add the onions. Let cool 15 minutes. Beat in the eggs. Fold in the noodles. Taste for seasoning. Pour into a well-buttered 9-inch mold. Set in a pan of water.

Bake in a 350° oven 35 minutes, or until the mixture is set. Run a knife around the edge and carefully unmold. The center may be filled with creamed fish or vegetables.

Serves 4–6.

CHEESE AND NOODLE LOAF

2 tablespoons butter
2 tablespoons flour
1½ cups milk
1 teaspoon salt
Dash cayenne pepper
1 teaspoon paprika

1 cup grated cheddar
    cheese
3 eggs
½ pound fine noodles,
    cooked and drained

Melt the butter in a saucepan; blend in the flour. Gradually add the milk, stirring constantly to the boiling point. Cook over low heat 5 minutes. Add the salt, cayenne pepper, paprika, and cheese, stirring steadily until the cheese melts.

Beat the eggs in a bowl; gradually add the cheese sauce, mixing constantly to prevent curdling. Fold in the noodles. Pour into a buttered 10-inch loaf pan.

Bake in a 350° oven 35 minutes, or until firm. Turn out carefully onto a platter and serve in slices.

Serves 4–6.

POLISH DUMPLINGS

(Pierogi)

2 cups cottage cheese, drained	½ cup sifted flour
4 egg yolks	½ teaspoon salt
1 tablespoon melted butter	2 teaspoons sugar
	4 egg whites

Force the cheese through a sieve. Beat in the egg yolks until smooth and light. Add the butter, flour, salt, and sugar; mix well. Beat the egg whites until stiff but not dry and fold into the cheese mixture.

Drop by the tablespoon into deep rapidly boiling salted water. Cook until dumplings rise to the top. Drain well. Serve with sugar, cinnamon, and sour cream.

Serves 4–6.

PIEROGI WITH CREAM CHEESE

2 cups sifted flour	¼ pound cream cheese
½ teaspoon salt	4 tablespoons sugar
3 eggs	1 tablespoon melted butter
½ cup water	½ teaspoon vanilla
½ cup cottage cheese	

Sift the flour and salt onto a board and make a well in the center. Into it put 2 eggs and the water. Work in the flour, kneading until a dough is formed. Cover with a bowl and let stand for 15 minutes.

Beat together the remaining egg, cottage cheese, cream cheese, sugar, butter, and vanilla until smooth and fluffy.

Roll out the dough as thin as possible on a lightly floured board. Cut into 3-inch circles. Place a teaspoonful of the cheese mixture on each. Fold over the dough, sealing the edges well.

Drop into deep boiling salted water. Boil until the *pierogi* rise to the surface, about 10 minutes. Drain well. Serve with melted butter and sour cream.

Serves 4–6.

CHEESE NOODLES

½ *pound (2 sticks) butter*
½ *pound cottage cheese,*
    well drained
2 *eggs*
1 *teaspoon salt*

2½ *cups sifted flour*
½ *cup melted butter*
½ *cup grated Parmesan*
    cheese

Cream the butter until light and fluffy. Beat in the cottage cheese, eggs, and salt. Mix in the flour gradually, adding just enough to form a dough. It may not be necessary to add all the flour.

Roll out as thin as possible on a lightly floured board. Cut into strips ¼ inch wide and 2 inches long. Let dry on the board for 4 hours.

Drop into boiling salted water. Boil 10 minutes. Drain well. Serve with melted butter and Parmesan cheese.

Serves 4.

CHEESE KREPLACH

2 *cups sifted flour*	1 *egg, beaten*
3 *egg yolks*	1 *teaspoon sugar*
¾ *teaspoon salt*	1 *teaspoon grated lemon*
¼ *cup warm water*	*rind (optional)*
(approximately)	3 *tablespoons melted butter*
1 *pound cottage cheese*	

Sift the flour onto a board. Make a well in the center. In it put the egg yolks, ¼ teaspoon of the salt, and 3 tablespoons of the water. Work in the flour and knead until a stiff dough is formed, adding a little more water if necessary. Knead until smooth and elastic. Cover the dough and let stand for 15 minutes. Roll out the dough as thin as possible. Cut into 3-inch squares.

Mix together the cottage cheese, egg, sugar, lemon rind, melted butter, and remaining salt. Place a heaping teaspoonful of the mixture on each square. Fold the dough over diagonally to form a triangle and press the edges together carefully.

Drop into deep boiling salted water. Boil rapidly 10 minutes. Drain well. Serve with melted butter and sour cream, if desired. *Serves 6–8.*

NOODLE PIZZAS

1 *egg*	¼ *pound mozzarella*
1 *tablespoon water*	*cheese, thinly sliced*
2 *cups French-Fried*	½ *cup grated Parmesan*
Noodles (see recipe)	*cheese*
2½ *cups Tomato Sauce*	
(see recipe)	

Beat the egg and water; pour over the fried noodles and mix lightly. Shape into 2-inch rounds ⅛ inch thick. Arrange on a well-oiled baking sheet. Bake in a 250° oven 15 minutes, or until dry to the touch. Loosen from the pan with a spatula immediately.

Cover each noodle round with Tomato Sauce and a piece of mozzarella cheese. Sprinkle tops with the Parmesan cheese. Bake in a 350° oven 10 minutes, or until lightly browned and cheese is melted.

Makes about 32.

NOTE: Anchovies or sausages may also be arranged over the sauce.

VERMICELLI WITH CHEESE SAUCE
(Vermicelli al Formaggio)

1 *pound ricotta cheese*	1 *teaspoon salt*
3 *tablespoons grated*	½ *teaspoon white pepper*
Parmesan cheese	1 *pound vermicelli or fine*
3 *tablespoons olive oil*	*noodles, cooked and*
1 *cup hot water*	*drained*

Beat together the ricotta cheese and Parmesan, then gradually add the oil. Very gradually beat in the water, then mix in the salt and pepper. Pour over the hot vermicelli and toss to coat well.

Serves 4–6.

With Eggs and Soufflés

*E*ggs are usually considered a breakfast food. Prepared with *pasta*, they can be served at any meal. This method of egg cookery is particularly recommended to people who don't like eggs. Eggs provide the much-needed proteins, and with *pasta* are delicious and satisfying.

TIMBALE OF SPAGHETTI

2 tablespoons butter	¼ teaspoon dry mustard
2 tablespoons flour	1 cup grated Gruyère
1½ cups milk	cheese
1 teaspoon salt	3 eggs, beaten
¼ teaspoon pepper	½ pound spaghetti, cooked,
½ teaspoon paprika	drained, and chopped

Melt the butter in a saucepan. Blend in the flour. Gradually add the milk, stirring constantly to the boiling point. Stir in the salt, pepper, paprika, mustard, and cheese. Cook over low heat 5 minutes. Cool 10 minutes. Beat in the eggs, then mix in the spaghetti. Taste for seasoning.

Pour mixture into a buttered 2-quart soufflé dish. Place in a pan and add enough hot water to reach halfway up the sides of the soufflé dish. Bake in a 350° oven 30 minutes, or until set.

Serves 4.

CHEESE AND NOODLE OMELET

(Tortilla de Tallarines y Queso)

6 eggs
1 cup grated Parmesan
   cheese
1 teaspoon salt
¼ teaspoon freshly ground
   black pepper

3 cups noodles broken into
   small pieces, cooked
   and drained
4 tablespoons butter

Beat the eggs in a bowl. Mix in the cheese, salt, pepper, and noodles.

Melt 2 tablespoons of the butter in a skillet. Fry 2 tablespoonfuls of the mixture at a time until brown on both sides. Add more butter as required. Keep the little omelets in a warm oven until serving time.

Serves 6–8.

SLOVENIAN MACARONI

1 16-ounce can tomatoes
2 teaspoons salt
½ teaspoon freshly ground
   black pepper
1 pound macaroni, cooked
   and drained

½ cup melted butter
½ cup grated Gruyère or
   Swiss cheese
3 eggs
2 cups heavy cream

Force the tomatoes through a sieve or purée in an electric blender. Add 1 teaspoon of the salt and ¼ teaspoon of the pepper. Cook over low heat 10 minutes, stirring occasionally.

Spread half the macaroni in a buttered baking dish. Pour half the melted butter over it. Cover with the tomatoes and half the cheese. Spread the remaining macaroni on top. Beat the eggs in a bowl; mix in the cream and remaining salt and pepper. Pour over the macaroni. Sprinkle the remaining melted butter and cheese on top. Bake in a 375° oven 30 minutes, or until custard is set.

Serves 4–6.

MACARONI WITH SCRAMBLED EGGS

¼ *pound butter*
½ *cup grated Parmesan cheese*
1 *pound macaroni, cooked and drained*
5 *eggs*

3 *tablespoons heavy cream*
1½ *teaspoons salt*
¼ *teaspoon freshly ground black pepper*
2 *cups cooked or canned green peas*

Melt the butter in a saucepan. Add the cheese and macaroni. Toss until macaroni is coated with the butter.

Beat the eggs, cream, salt, and pepper in a bowl. Add the green peas, then combine with the macaroni.

Cook over low heat, stirring constantly, until the eggs begin to set. Do not overcook. Serve sprinkled with additional cheese, if desired.

Serves 4–6.

MACARONI WITH EGG CURRY

4 *tablespoons butter*
4 *tablespoons flour*
2 *cups milk*
1 *teaspoon salt*
¼ *teaspoon freshly ground black pepper*

1 *tablespoon curry powder*
½ *pound macaroni, cooked and drained*
6 *hard-cooked eggs, quartered*

Melt the butter in a saucepan. Blend in the flour. Gradually add the milk, stirring constantly to the boiling point. Mix in the salt, pepper, and curry powder. Cook over low heat 5 minutes.

Arrange 6 individual mounds of macaroni and make a depression in each. Place 4 egg quarters in each and pour the curry sauce on top.

Serves 6.

SPAGHETTI-EGG CASSEROLE

1 10½-ounce can con-
    densed tomato soup
1 cup milk
¾ cup grated cheddar
    cheese
1½ teaspoons salt

½ teaspoon pepper
¾ pound spaghetti, cooked
    and drained
6 eggs
3 tablespoons butter

Mix the soup and milk in a saucepan until smooth. Add the cheese and cook over low heat, stirring frequently until the cheese melts. Mix in ½ teaspoon of the salt and ¼ teaspoon of the pepper.

Spread the spaghetti on the bottom of a buttered baking dish. Make 6 evenly spaced depressions with the back of a spoon. Break an egg into each. Sprinkle with the remaining salt and pepper. Dot the spaghetti with the butter. Pour the sauce over all.

Bake in a 375° oven 10 minutes, or until the eggs are set.

Serves 3–6.

NOTE: If desired, individual baking dishes may be used.

EGG AND NOODLE CASSEROLE

3 tablespoons butter
3 tablespoons grated onion
3 tablespoons flour
2 cups milk
1 teaspoon salt
¼ teaspoon pepper
2 cups (½ pound) grated
   American cheese

½ pound medium noodles,
   cooked and drained
6 hard-cooked eggs, halved
1 cup soft bread crumbs
4 tablespoons melted
   butter

Melt the butter in a saucepan; sauté the onion for 2 minutes. Blend in the flour. Add the milk, stirring constantly to the boiling point, then cook over low heat 5 minutes. Mix in the salt, pepper, and cheese until the cheese melts.

Combine the noodles with half of the sauce. Pour into a buttered casserole. Arrange the halves of eggs over the noodles. Pour the remaining sauce on top, and sprinkle with the bread crumbs and melted butter.

Bake in a 350° oven 20 minutes.

Serves 4–6.

NOODLES POLONAISE

4 tablespoons butter
1 pound fine noodles,
   cooked and drained
1 cup sour cream
2 teaspoons salt
¼ teaspoon freshly ground
   black pepper

3 hard-cooked eggs,
   chopped
2 tablespoons chopped
   parsley
4 tablespoons grated
   Parmesan cheese
1 tablespoon bread crumbs

Melt the butter in a saucepan. Add the noodles, tossing lightly. Add the sour cream, salt, and pepper. Toss again. Turn into a but-

tered baking dish. Place under the broiler until lightly browned.
Sprinkle with the eggs, parsley, cheese, and bread crumbs.

Serves 4.

HAM AND CHEESE CUSTARD

5 egg yolks, beaten
1 teaspoon salt
¼ teaspoon pepper
2 cups grated Swiss cheese
½ pound boiled ham,
    ground

2 tablespoons chopped
    parsley
½ pound egg flakes (small
    square egg noodles),
    cooked and drained
5 egg whites

Combine the egg yolks, salt, pepper, Swiss cheese, ham, and
parsley. Stir in the egg flakes.

Beat the egg whites until stiff but not dry. Fold carefully into
the noodle mixture. Pour into a buttered 2-quart casserole or
soufflé dish. Bake in a 375° oven for 35 minutes.

Serves 4–6.

HAM-NOODLE SOUFFLE

3 tablespoons butter
2 tablespoons flour
1¼ cups beef broth
¼ teaspoon freshly ground
    black pepper
4 egg yolks
¼ cup minced, sautéed
    mushrooms

1 cup finely ground cooked
    ham
4 egg whites
¼ pound fine noodles,
    cooked and drained
2 tablespoons melted
    butter

Melt the butter in a skillet; blend in the flour. Gradually add the
broth, stirring constantly to the boiling point, then cook over low
heat 5 minutes, stirring occasionally. Stir in the pepper.

Beat the egg yolks in a bowl; gradually add the hot mixture, beating constantly to prevent curdling. Mix in the mushrooms and ham. Taste for seasoning. Cool 10 minutes.

Beat the egg whites until stiff but not dry. Fold them into the mushroom-ham mixture carefully and gently. Spread the noodles in a buttered 2-quart soufflé dish or casserole. Pour the melted butter, then the soufflé mixture over the noodles. Place the soufflé dish in a shallow pan of hot water. Bake in a preheated 400° oven 35 minutes. Serve immediately, or the soufflé will fall.

Serves 4.

NOODLE SOUFFLE

(Soufflé di Tagliolini)

¼ *pound butter*
3 *tablespoons flour*
1¼ *teaspoons salt*
¼ *teaspoon white pepper*
2 *cups milk*
½ *cup heavy cream*

½ *cup grated Parmesan*
  cheese
3 *egg yolks*
½ *pound fine noodles,*
  cooked and drained
5 *egg whites, stiffly beaten*

Melt half of the butter in a saucepan; blend in the flour, salt, and pepper. Add the milk and cream, stirring steadily to the boiling point, then cook over low heat 5 minutes. Mix in the cheese and remaining butter until melted.

Beat the egg yolks in a bowl; gradually add the hot sauce, stirring steadily to prevent curdling. Mix in the noodles; taste for seasoning. Cool 15 minutes, then fold in the beaten egg whites. Turn into a buttered 2-quart soufflé dish. Bake in a preheated 375° oven 25 minutes, or until browned and set.

Serves 4–6.

CHEESE AND MACARONI SOUFFLE

3 tablespoons butter
2 tablespoons chopped
   onions
3 tablespoons flour
1 cup milk, scalded
1 teaspoon salt
½ teaspoon freshly ground
   black pepper
Dash cayenne pepper

2 tablespoons chopped
   pimiento
4 egg yolks
1 cup grated cheddar
   cheese
¼ cup sliced, sautéed
   mushrooms
¼ pound macaroni, cooked
   and drained
4 egg whites

Melt the butter in a saucepan. Sauté the onions 5 minutes, stirring frequently. Blend in the flour. Add the milk gradually, stirring constantly to the boiling point, then cook over low heat 5 minutes, stirring occasionally. Mix in the salt, pepper, cayenne pepper, and pimiento.

Beat the egg yolks in a bowl until light. Gradually add the hot sauce, stirring constantly. Mix in the cheese, mushrooms, and macaroni. Taste for seasoning. Let cool for 10 minutes.

Beat the egg whites until stiff but not dry; fold into the cheese mixture carefully. Pour into a buttered 1½-quart soufflé dish. Bake in a preheated 350° oven 35 minutes. Serve immediately.

Serves 4–6.

In Soups

Soup has always been a hearty dish, and every country has a soup specialty. Italian soups are famous for their delicious combinations of dried beans and macaroni. The Chinese serve both plain and delectable stuffed noodles in clear broth, but no matter what the origin is, there is no doubt that *pasta* in soup is delicious and filling. Soup makes a wonderful lunch or supper when served with crusty bread and cheese. Make extra amounts and freeze some for future use.

SPAGHETTI IN BROTH

(Spaghetti in Brodetto)

¼ pound (1 stick) butter
1 pound mushrooms, sliced
3 tablespoons flour
1 cup dry white wine
3 cups chicken or beef
    broth
1 teaspoon salt

½ teaspoon freshly ground
    black pepper
2 tablespoons lemon juice
3 egg yolks
2 tablespoons chopped
    parsley
1 pound spaghetti, cooked
    and drained

Melt the butter in a saucepan; sauté the mushrooms 10 minutes, stirring frequently. Blend in the flour. Add the wine gradually, stirring constantly to the boiling point. Add the broth, salt, and pepper, mixing steadily. Cook over low heat 30 minutes.

Beat the lemon juice, egg yolks, and parsley together in a bowl. Very gradually add the mushroom mixture, beating steadily to prevent curdling. Correct seasoning.

Return the mixture to the saucepan and reheat, but do not allow it to boil. Add the spaghetti and toss lightly. Serve immediately. *Serves 4–6.*

MACARONI-VEGETABLE SOUP

(Minestra di Pasta e Legumbres)

2 *cups dried kidney beans*	1 *29-ounce can tomatoes*
2 *quarts water*	1 *cup beef broth*
¼ *cup olive oil*	½ *pound elbow macaroni*
1 *cup chopped onions*	1½ *teaspoons salt*
1 *clove garlic, minced*	¼ *teaspoon dried ground*
2 *cups shredded cabbage*	*red peppers*
2 *carrots, chopped*	*Grated Parmesan cheese*

Wash the beans. Cover with water, bring to a boil, and let soak 1 hour. Drain.

Combine the beans and the 2 quarts of water in a saucepan. Bring to a boil. Cover and cook over low heat 1 hour.

Heat the oil in a skillet; sauté the onions and garlic 10 minutes. Add to the beans with the cabbage, carrots, tomatoes, and broth. Bring to a boil and cook over low heat 45 minutes.

Pour boiling water over the macaroni and let soak 10 minutes. Drain. Add macaroni, salt, and peppers to the soup. Cook over low heat 15 minutes. Taste for seasoning. Serve with grated cheese.

Serves 8–10.

VEGETABLE SOUP
(Minestrone)

1 *cup dried chick-peas*
3 *tablespoons olive oil*
¾ *cup chopped onions*
2 *cloves garlic, minced*
¼ *cup chopped celery*
½ *cup diced carrots*
1½ *cups diced zucchini*
1 *cup diced potatoes*
1½ *cups coarsely chopped*
cabbage

2 *tablespoons tomato*
paste
8 *cups boiling water*
2 *teaspoons salt*
½ *teaspoon freshly ground*
black pepper
½ *teaspoon basil*
2 *tablespoons minced*
parsley
1 *cup cooked macaroni*
Grated Parmesan cheese

Wash the chick-peas. Cover with water and bring to a boil. Let soak 1 hour. Drain, add fresh water to cover, and cook over medium heat 1½ hours. Drain. (Use 2 cups canned chick-peas if you prefer, in which case no cooking is required.)

Heat the oil in a saucepan; sauté the onions, garlic, and celery 5 minutes. Mix in the carrots, zucchini, potatoes, and cabbage; cook 5 minutes. Stir in the tomato paste, then add the water, salt, pepper, and basil. Bring to a boil; cover and cook over low heat 1 hour. Mix in the parsley and macaroni; cook 5 minutes and taste for seasoning. Serve with grated Parmesan cheese.

Serves 6–8.

QUICK MINESTRONE

¼ cup olive oil
1 cup chopped onions
2 potatoes, peeled and
    diced
1 cup canned tomatoes
3 cups beef broth
3 cups water
1 package frozen mixed
    vegetables

½ pound vermicelli, broken
    into 2-inch lengths
2 teaspoons salt
½ teaspoon freshly ground
    black pepper
½ cup grated Parmesan
    cheese

Heat the olive oil in a sauccpan; sauté the onions 10 minutes.
Add the potatoes, tomatoes, broth, and water. Bring to a boil;
cover and cook over medium heat 10 minutes. Add the mixed
vegetables, vermicelli, salt, and pepper. Cook over low heat 25
minutes. Taste for seasoning. Serve with the grated cheese.
Serves 6–8.

VEGETABLE-MACARONI SOUP, GENOA STYLE

(Minestrone alla Genovese)

2 tablespoons olive oil
1 cup grated carrots
1 cup chopped onions
2 leeks, sliced
2 cups peeled, diced
    potatoes
2 cups shredded spinach
2 quarts water
3 cups cooked or canned
    kidney beans
2 teaspoons salt

½ teaspoon freshly ground
    black pepper
3 tablespoons minced
    parsley
½ teaspoon basil
2 cloves garlic, minced
4 slices bacon, diced
1½ cups macaroni
Grated Pecorino or Parme-
    san cheese

Heat the oil in a saucepan; add the carrots, onions, leeks, potatoes, and spinach and cook 5 minutes. Add the water, beans, salt,

and pepper; bring to a boil and cook over low heat 1 hour. In an electric blender, purée the parsley, basil, garlic, and bacon (add a little soup), or pound ingredients to a paste, using a mortar and pestle. Add to the soup with the macaroni. Cook 20 minutes, or until macaroni is tender. Serve with grated Pecorino or Parmesan cheese.

Serves 6–8.

BEAN-NOODLE SOUP, GENOA STYLE

(Minestra Genovese di Fagiolini al Pesto)

2 *cups dried navy beans*	2 *slices bacon, diced*
2½ *quarts water*	1 *clove garlic, minced*
1½ *cups peeled, diced*	2 *tablespoons minced*
potatoes	*parsley*
1 *stalk celery, diced*	½ *teaspoon basil*
1 *leek, thinly sliced*	1 *tablespoon olive oil*
1 *cup grated carrots*	2 *tablespoons grated*
1½ *teaspoons salt*	*Parmesan cheese*
½ *teaspoon freshly ground*	1 *cup uncooked broad*
black pepper	*noodles*

Wash the beans. Cover with water and bring to a boil. Let soak 1 hour. Drain. Add the 2½ quarts of water, bring to a boil, and cook over low heat 2½ hours. Add the potatoes, celery, leek, carrots, salt, and pepper; cook 30 minutes.

In an electric blender, purée the bacon, garlic, parsley, basil, olive oil, and cheese (add a little soup), or pound ingredients to a paste, using a mortar and pestle. Add to the soup; cook 10 minutes. Mix in the noodles; cook 10 minutes longer.

Serves 6–8.

MACARONI AND CHICK-PEA SOUP

(Minestra di Pasta)

¼ *cup olive oil*
3 *cloves garlic, minced*
6 *anchovy fillets, drained and minced*
1 *cup chopped parsley*
2 *20-ounce cans chick-peas*
4 *cups water*

1½ *cups peeled, chopped tomatoes*
¼ *teaspoon freshly ground black pepper*
1 *teaspoon rosemary*
1 *pound elbow macaroni, cooked and drained*
Grated Parmesan cheese

Heat the oil in a saucepan; sauté the garlic, anchovies, and parsley 3 minutes, stirring frequently. Add the undrained chick-peas, the water, tomatoes, pepper, and rosemary.

Bring to a boil; cover and cook over low heat 30 minutes, stirring frequently. Taste for seasoning and mix in the macaroni. Cook 5 minutes. The resulting soup will be very thick. Serve with a bowl of grated Parmesan cheese.

Serves 4–8.

TOMATO-VEGETABLE SOUP WITH HERBS

(Soupe au Pistou)

½ cup olive oil
1½ cups chopped onions
8 cups water
¾ pound green beans, cut
  into 1-inch lengths
3 potatoes, peeled and
  cubed
3 tomatoes, peeled and
  cubed
¼ pound vermicelli, broken
  in half

1½ teaspoons salt
¼ teaspoon freshly ground
  black pepper
2 tablespoons fresh basil
  or 1 teaspoon dried
3 cloves garlic, minced
1 tablespoon tomato
  paste
½ cup grated Parmesan
  cheese

Heat half of the olive oil in a large saucepan. Sauté the onions
15 minutes, stirring frequently. Add the water, beans, potatoes, and
tomatoes. Cook over medium heat 15 minutes. Mix in the vermicelli, salt, and pepper. Cook over low heat 15 minutes.

If dried basil is used, soak it in hot water 10 minutes, then drain.
Pound the garlic into a paste. Add the basil and pound until very
smooth. Mix in the tomato paste. Gradually add the remaining
oil, mixing steadily. Serve the soup with a tablespoon of the garlic
mixture in each plate and with grated cheese.

Serves 8–10.

VERMICELLI-MUSHROOM SOUP

(Vermicelli à la Bourbonnaise)

4 tablespoons butter
½ pound mushrooms, sliced
½ pound vermicelli, broken
  into pieces

3 cups chicken broth
1½ teaspoons salt

Melt the butter in a saucepan; sauté the mushrooms 5 minutes. Add the vermicelli. Cook, stirring almost constantly, until the vermicelli browns.

Add the broth and salt. Cook 6 minutes, or until the vermicelli is tender.

Serves 2–4.

CARAWAY AND NOODLE SOUP

4 tablespoons butter	⅛ teaspoon freshly ground
4 tablespoons flour	black pepper
7 cups beef broth	¼ pound broad noodles,
1 tablespoon caraway seeds	cooked and drained
	Sour cream

Melt the butter in a saucepan. Stir in the flour until smooth and browned. Gradually add the broth, stirring constantly until the boiling point. Mix in the caraway seeds and pepper. Cook over low heat 10 minutes. Add the noodles. Cook 5 minutes. Taste for seasoning. Serve with a spoonful of sour cream.

Serves 6–8.

EGG NOODLE SOUP

2 eggs	6 cups boiling chicken or
½ teaspoon salt	beef broth
2 cups sifted flour	2 tablespoons parsley or
½ cup oil or shortening	chives

Beat the eggs and salt in a bowl. Add the flour, mixing lightly until a dough is formed. Roll out as thin as possible on a lightly floured surface. Cut into 7-inch circles.

Heat 3 tablespoons of the oil in a 7-inch skillet. Fry one piece of dough at a time until lightly browned on both sides. Add additional oil as required. Cool. Cut into narrow strips.

Add the noodle strips to the broth and cook over low heat 15 minutes. Sprinkle with parsley or chives.

Serves 6–8.

DUTCH MILK SOUP WITH RIBBONS
(Melksnysels)

1⅛ *cups sifted flour*	3 *egg yolks*
¼ *teaspoon salt*	¼ *teaspoon sugar*
½ *teaspoon baking powder*	½ *teaspoon cinnamon*
2 *quarts milk*	3 *egg whites*

Sift 1 cup of the flour with the salt and baking powder into a bowl. Gradually add about ½ cup of the milk, using just enough to make a stiff dough. Knead until the dough is elastic and smooth. Roll out as thin as possible on a lightly floured surface. Let stand 15 minutes. Sprinkle with the remaining flour, and roll up lightly like a jelly roll. Cut evenly into ¼-inch slices. Bring the remaining milk to an active boil in a deep saucepan. Drop the noodle ribbons into it, and cook until they come to the top. Drain, reserving the milk, and keep noodles warm.

Beat the egg yolks, sugar, and cinnamon in a bowl. Gradually add 1 cup of the hot milk, beating constantly to prevent curdling. Return to the remaining milk, stirring constantly. Heat, but do not allow to boil. Beat the egg whites until stiff but not dry. Pour the milk mixture over them, mixing gently. Place the noodles in bowls or soup plates, and pour the custard mixture over them. Serve hot.

Serves 8–10.

GREEN SOUP

3 tablespoons butter
1 cup chopped green onions
1 package frozen green peas,
   thawed
1 package frozen spinach,
   thawed
2 cups chopped lettuce

2 tablespoons chopped
   parsley
6 cups water
2 teaspoons salt
1 cup milk
¼ pound elbow macaroni,
   cooked and drained

Heat the butter in a saucepan. Sauté the green onions over very low heat 15 minutes. Add green peas, spinach, lettuce, parsley, water, and salt. Cook over low heat 20 minutes. Purée in an electric blender or force through a sieve. Return to saucepan. Mix in the milk and macaroni. Cook over low heat 5 minutes. Taste for seasoning.
Serves 6–8.

LENTIL AND MACARONI SOUP

1 cup lentils
2 quarts water
1 pound smoked ham
2 stalks celery, sliced
⅛ teaspoon dried ground
   red peppers

3 tablespoons olive oil
2 onions, chopped
½ cup elbow macaroni,
   cooked and drained

Wash the lentils thoroughly. Combine with the water, ham, celery, and dried red peppers in a saucepan. Bring to a boil and cook over low heat 1½ hours. Remove the ham and cut into small cubes. Force the lentils through a sieve or purée in an electric blender. Return to the saucepan.

Heat the olive oil in a skillet; sauté the onions 10 minutes, stirring frequently. Add to the saucepan with the cubed ham and macaroni; cook 10 minutes.

Serves 6–8.

LEEK-CABBAGE SOUP

(Potage Villageoise)

4 *tablespoons butter*	¼ *teaspoon white pepper*
6 *leeks, sliced*	2 *tablespoons flour*
3 *cups shredded cabbage*	1 *cup heavy cream*
6 *cups water*	¼ *pound vermicelli, half*
1½ *teaspoons salt*	*cooked and drained*

Melt the butter in a saucepan. Sauté the leeks and cabbage 15 minutes, stirring frequently, but do not allow to brown. Add the water, salt, and pepper. Cook over low heat 45 minutes, stirring occasionally. Mix the flour and cream together and add, stirring constantly to the boiling point. Mix in the vermicelli; cook over low heat 10 minutes. Taste for seasoning.

Serves 6–8.

BROCCOLI AND MACARONI SOUP

(Zuppa di Broccoli)

2 *strips salt pork, chopped fine*	¼ *teaspoon black pepper*
2 *tablespoons olive oil*	3 *cups broccoli flowerets or 1 package frozen*
1 *clove garlic, minced*	2 *cups short macaroni*
3 *tablespoons tomato paste*	⅓ *cup grated Parmesan cheese*
6 *cups water*	
1 *teaspoon salt*	

Brown the salt pork in a saucepan; pour off most of the fat. Add the oil, garlic, tomato paste, water, salt, and pepper. Bring to a boil and cook over low heat 20 minutes. Add the broccoli; cover and cook 5 minutes. Mix in the macaroni and cook 10 minutes longer. Serve with the cheese.

Serves 4–5.

GOULASH SOUP

2 tablespoons butter
1½ cups chopped onions
1½ pounds beef, cut into
    ½-inch cubes
Beef-bone
  8 cups boiling water
  2 teaspoons salt
⅛ teaspoon freshly ground
    black pepper
  2 teaspoons paprika

2 green peppers, cut
    julienne
2 tomatoes, chopped
2 carrots, sliced thin
2 potatoes, peeled and
    cubed
½ pound broad noodles,
    half cooked and
    drained

Melt the butter in a saucepan. Sauté the onions 5 minutes, stirring frequently. Add the beef and brown well on all sides. Add the bone, water, salt, pepper, and paprika. Cook over medium heat 30 minutes. Add the green peppers, tomatoes, and carrots. Cover and cook over low heat 1 hour. Add the potatoes and cook 10 minutes. Mix in the noodles and cook 10 minutes longer. Taste for seasoning.

Serve in deep soup plates or bowls, with several pieces of meat in each.

Serves 6–8.

MEAT BALL AND VERMICELLI SOUP

¼ *pound thin Chinese*
  noodles or vermicelli
2 *tablespoons cornstarch*
¼ *cup water*
½ *pound ground pork*
1 *teaspoon salt*

¼ *teaspoon pepper*
4 *tablespoons oil*
6 *cups beef broth*
2 *tablespoons soy sauce*
¼ *cup sliced green onions*

Break the noodles into 2-inch lengths. Cover with boiling water and let soak 5 minutes; drain well.

Mix together the cornstarch and water. Add the pork, salt, and pepper and mix well. Shape into walnut-sized balls. Fry in hot oil until browned on all sides.

Bring the broth to a boil; add the noodles and cook 5 minutes. Carefully drop the meat balls into the broth and cook 5 minutes. Stir in the soy sauce and green onions. Cook 3 minutes.

Serves 6–8.

NOODLE SOUP WITH LIVERS

(Pasta in Brodo con Fegatini)

½ *pound chicken livers*
3 *tablespoons butter*
½ *teaspoon salt*
6 *cups chicken broth*

1½ *cups cooked, drained*
  fine noodles
1 *cup firmly cooked green*
  peas
Grated Parmesan cheese

Wash the livers, cutting away any discolored spots. Chop the livers coarsely and sauté in the butter 3 minutes; season with the salt.

Bring the broth to a boil; add the livers, noodles, and green peas. Cook over low heat 2 minutes. Taste for seasoning and serve with the grated cheese.

Serves 6–8.

CLAM CHOWDER, ALASKAN STYLE

36 clams and their juice,
   or 2 cans minced clams
4 tablespoons butter
1 cup grated onions
1 clove garlic, minced
3 tablespoons flour
3 cups milk

1 bay leaf
¼ teaspoon freshly ground
   black pepper
2 tablespoons chopped
   parsley
½ pound noodles, half
   cooked and drained

Grind the clams and drain, reserving the juice. Add enough water to make 1 quart. Set aside.

Melt the butter in a saucepan; sauté the onions and garlic 10 minutes, stirring frequently. Blend in the flour. Gradually add the clam-juice mixture, stirring constantly to the boiling point. Mix in the milk, bay leaf, pepper, and parsley. Cook over low heat 20 minutes. Discard the bay leaf. Add the clams and noodles. Cook 5 minutes. Taste for seasoning.

Serves 6–8.

SPANISH VERMICELLI SOUP

¼ pound (1 stick) butter
½ pound vermicelli,
   broken into pieces
1½ cups finely chopped
   onions
3 cups chopped tomatoes
3 tablespoons chopped
   parsley

7 cups chicken broth
1 teaspoon salt
¼ teaspoon dried ground
   chili peppers
⅛ teaspoon saffron
½ cup grated Parmesan
   cheese

Melt the butter in a saucepan. Add the vermicelli and sauté until brown, stirring frequently. Remove the vermicelli.

Add the onions to the butter remaining in the saucepan; sauté 10 minutes, stirring frequently. Mix in the tomatoes, parsley, broth,

salt, and chili peppers. Cover and cook over low heat 15 minutes. Add the vermicelli and cook 20 minutes. Dissolve the saffron in a spoonful of hot soup and stir in with the cheese. Cook 2 minutes.
  Serves 6–8.

ITALIAN BEAN AND MACARONI SOUP

1½ *cups dried white beans*
1 *marrow bone*
1 *cup chopped onion*
4 *quarts water*
¼ *cup olive oil*
3 *cloves garlic, minced*
1 *tablespoon tomato*
  paste

1 *tablespoon salt*
½ *teaspoon freshly ground*
  black pepper
½ *teaspoon orégano*
1 *cup elbow macaroni or*
  small shells

Wash the beans; cover with water and bring to a boil. Remove from the heat and let soak 1 hour. Drain. Add the bone, onion, and the 4 quarts water; bring to a boil and cook over low heat 1½ hours. Remove the bone, scooping out any remaining marrow, and return marrow to soup. Purée 1 cup of beans in an electric blender or force through a food mill; return to soup.

Heat the oil in a skillet. Sauté the garlic 2 minutes; stir in the tomato paste. Cook over low heat 5 minutes. Add to the soup with the salt, pepper, and orégano. Cook over low heat 1½ hours. Add the macaroni; cook 20 minutes. Taste for seasoning.
  Serves 10–12.

KOREAN NOODLE SOUP WITH MEAT BALLS

(Kook Soo)

4 tablespoons vegetable oil
1 onion, sliced
3 cloves garlic, minced
⅓ cup chopped green onions
4 tomatoes, chopped
6 cups beef broth
½ teaspoon pepper
2 tablespoons soy sauce
¼ pound vermicelli, half
    cooked and drained

1 pound ground beef
1½ teaspoons salt
Dash of cayenne pepper
½ teaspoon ginger
2 tablespoons ground
    sesame seeds
¼ cup flour
1 egg, beaten

Heat 2 tablespoons of the oil in a saucepan. Add the onion, garlic, and green onions. Sauté 10 minutes. Add the tomatoes, beef broth, and pepper. Cook over low heat 20 minutes. Add the soy sauce and the vermicelli. Cook 10 minutes.

Mix together the ground beef, salt, cayenne pepper, ginger, and sesame seeds. Form into walnut-sized balls. Dip into the flour and then the egg.

Heat the remaining oil in a skillet. Fry the meat balls until browned on all sides. Place the meat balls in the soup and serve.
Serves 6–8.

SAIGON BEEF-NOODLE SOUP
(Pho)

2 *pounds beef*
3 *onions*
2 *cloves garlic*
3 *quarts water*
1 *tablespoon salt*
¼ *teaspoon white pepper*

1 *teaspoon anchovy paste*
1 *teaspoon vinegar*
1 *cup flour*
1 *egg*
¼ *cup water*

Combine the meat, onions, garlic, water, salt, and pepper and cook over medium heat 2 hours. Strain. Stir in the anchovy paste and vinegar.

Mix the flour, egg, and water together; knead until very smooth. Force the mixture through a colander into the boiling soup. Cook 10 minutes, or until noodles are tender. Cut the meat into small pieces and serve in the soup.

Serves 8–10.

CANTONESE NOODLES IN BROTH

½ *pound boneless pork*
4 *tablespoons vegetable oil*
¼ *cup thinly sliced green onions*
½ *pound spinach, washed, drained, and shredded*
3 *10½-ounce cans chicken broth*

3 *cups water*
2 *tablespoons soy sauce*
Chinese Noodles (see recipe) or ½ pound fine noodles, cooked and drained
1 *egg, beaten*

Cut the pork into matchlike pieces. Heat the oil in a 2-quart saucepan and brown the pork. Add the green onions and spinach;

cook 3 minutes, stirring frequently. Mix in the broth, water, and soy sauce. Bring to a boil and cook over low heat 5 minutes. Add the cooked, drained noodles; bring to an active boil and slowly stir in the egg until set.

Serves 6–8.

CHINESE NOODLE SOUP

(Tong Min)

1 *pound pork bones*
10 *cups water*
1 *onion*
½ *pound raw shrimp*
2 *teaspoons salt*
½ *cup chopped spinach*
½ *pound fine noodles
(Chinese, if available),
cooked and drained*

2 *teaspoons sesame-seed
oil or peanut oil*
2 *teaspoons soy sauce*
¼ *pound ham, cut julienne*
3 *green onions, chopped
fine*
2 *hard-cooked eggs,
coarsely chopped*
½ *teaspoon Ac'cent*

Wash the bones and combine in a saucepan with the water. Bring to a boil and skim the top. Add the onion, shrimp, salt, and spinach. Cook over medium heat 1½ hours. Strain and skim the fat.

Divide the noodles among 8–10 soup bowls. Sprinkle with a mixture of the oil and soy sauce. Pour soup over the noodles and garnish with the ham, green onions, eggs, and Ac'cent.

Serves 8–10.

CHINESE PORK DUMPLINGS IN SOUP
(Yow Jowton)

2½ cups sifted flour
3 eggs
½ teaspoon baking soda
2 tablespoons water
½ pound ground pork
¼ cup chopped
  mushrooms

2 teaspoons soy sauce
½ teaspoon salt
¼ teaspoon freshly ground
  black pepper
8 cups beef broth

Sift the flour onto a board. Make a well in the center and in it put the eggs and the baking soda dissolved in the water. Work in the flour, kneading until a stiff dough is formed. Cover and let stand 15 minutes.

Roll out the dough; fold over and roll out again, repeating the steps ten times. Roll out again as thin as possible. Cut into 2-inch squares.

Mix together the pork, mushrooms, soy sauce, salt, and pepper. Place a teaspoonful of the mixture on each square. Fold over and seal the edges well.

Drop into the boiling broth. Cook 20 minutes. Serve in the soup. *Serves 8.*

JAPANESE NOODLE-VEGETABLE SOUP

(Miso-Taki)

1½ cups cooked or canned
 lima beans or chick-
 peas
2 tablespoons vinegar
2 tablespoons beer
2 tablespoons soy sauce
1 tablespoon oil
½ cup chopped onions
6 cups beef broth

1 cup julienne-cut turnips
½ pound pork, cut julienne
1 teaspoon salt
¼ teaspoon pepper
½ pound medium egg
 noodles, cooked and
 drained
½ cup diced, cooked
 shrimp

Purée the beans in a blender or force through a sieve. Mix with the vinegar, beer, and soy sauce. Let stand 1 hour.

Heat the oil in a saucepan. Cook the onions 2 minutes. Stir in the bean mixture, broth, turnips, pork, salt, and pepper. Cook over low heat 15 minutes. Add the noodles and shrimp; cook 3 minutes.

Serves 4–6.

EGG PANCAKE NOODLES

(Fritatten)

4 eggs
⅔ cup milk
⅓ cup sifted flour

¼ teaspoon salt
2 tablespoons butter

Beat the eggs well; stir in the milk and beat in the flour and salt. Let stand 1 hour.

Melt 1 teaspoon butter in a 6-inch skillet. Pour in about 1 tablespoon of the batter, tilting the pan quickly to coat the bottom thinly. Bake until browned on both sides. Add butter to skillet as needed. Cool the pancakes, then cut into very narrow strips, like vermicelli. Serve in clear or vegetable soups.

Serves 6–8.

BAKED NOODLES FOR SOUP
(Mandlen)

2 *cups sifted flour*	3 *eggs*
1 *teaspoon salt*	2 *tablespoons vegetable oil*

Sift the flour and salt into a bowl. Beat the eggs and oil together and add, mixing lightly until a dough is formed.

Break off pieces of the dough and roll between floured hands into pencil-thin rolls. Cut into ½-inch lengths. Place on a cooky sheet.

Bake in a 375° oven 10 minutes, or until browned. Shake the pan occasionally.

Serve in chicken or beef soups.

Serves 8–10.

SPINACH PANCAKE NOODLES

4 *tablespoons butter*	½ *cup cooked chopped*
2 *tablespoons flour*	*spinach, drained*
2 *egg yolks*	½ *teaspoon salt*
	2 *egg whites, beaten stiff*

Cream 2 tablespoons of the butter; blend in the flour and egg yolks. Mix in the spinach and salt, then fold in the egg whites.

Melt 1 tablespoon butter in a 7-inch skillet; pour in half the mixture. Bake until dry and lightly browned on underside, then turn and bake other side until lightly browned. Turn out, roll up, and cut into narrow strips. Prepare second pancake. Serve in clear soups.

Serves 4–6.

Homemade Pasta

*I*т has been said that nothing is so soothing to a woman as the kneading motion. Today almost everyone buys bread and *pasta*, but there is no doubt that, properly handled, the homemade varieties are interesting, so try kneading your own noodle dough. Of course, if you prefer, there are dough hooks available for some electric mixers that will do the work for you. *Pasta* cutting machines roll the dough to a desired thickness and then cut it into different shapes.

EGG-NOODLE DOUGH
(Pasta al Uovo)

4 cups sifted flour   4 eggs
1 teaspoon salt   1 tablespoon vegetable oil

Sift the flour and salt onto a board. Make a well in the center and into it put the eggs and oil. Work in the flour with the fingers until a firm dough is formed. Then knead the dough until very smooth and elastic. This will take about 10–15 minutes. Cover the dough with a bowl and let it rest for 20 minutes. This makes it easier to roll.

Divide the dough into three pieces. Lightly flour a board and roll out the dough as thin as possible, the thinner the better. Cut as described below. If all the noodles are not to be used at once, store in a tightly closed container.

FETTUCCINE

Sprinkle the thinly rolled out dough lightly with flour cut into
½-inch-wide strips. Spread on a clean cloth and let dry for about
1 hour. Cook in a deep pot of boiling salted water. Drain well
and serve with a sauce or melted butter.

CANNELLONI

Cut the thinly rolled out dough into 4-inch squares. Don't dry
the dough. Cook a few squares at a time in deep boiling salted
water 2 minutes. Remove with a slotted spoon and drop into cold
salted water. Drain and dry on a cloth towel. Use as directed in
recipes.

LASAGNE

Sprinkle the thinly rolled out dough with flour. Cut into strips
6 inches long and 2 inches wide. Cook in deep boiling salted
water 4 minutes. Drain well and use as directed in recipes.

TAGLIATELLE

Prepare as for *fettuccine*, but cut into ¼-inch-wide strips.

NOODLE DOUGH

(Pasta Asciutta)

4 cups flour	1 tablespoon olive oil
3 eggs	Water

Sift the flour into a bowl; make a well in the center and into
it put the eggs and oil. Work in the flour until a dough is formed.
If too dry, add a little cold water. Pick up the dough and slap it
down hard a few times, then knead until very smooth and elastic.
This should take 10–15 minutes. Form into a ball and cover with a
bowl. Let stand 30 minutes. Roll out paper-thin and cut as desired.
This dough is used for *lasagne, ravioli, fettuccine,* etc.

CANNELLONI, RAVIOLI, AND TORTELLINI FILLINGS

MEAT

2 tablespoons butter	¼ cup grated Parmesan
1½ cups ground cooked	cheese
beef or veal	¼ cup dry bread crumbs
	⅛ teaspoon nutmeg

Melt the butter in a skillet; sauté the meat 5 minutes. Cool and mix in the cheese, bread crumbs, and nutmeg. Taste for seasoning.

SPINACH-MEAT

¾ cup cooked chopped	¼ cup grated Parmesan
spinach, drained	cheese
thoroughly	⅛ teaspoon nutmeg
¾ cup ground cooked meat	3 tablespoons dry bread
	crumbs

Mix all the ingredients together and taste for seasoning.

SPINACH-CHEESE

1 cup cooked chopped	¼ cup grated Parmesan
spinach, drained	cheese
thoroughly	3 tablespoons dry bread
½ cup ricotta or cottage	crumbs
cheese, drained	

Mix all the ingredients together and taste for seasoning.

BOLOGNESE

½ cup sausage meat
1 tablespoon butter
1 cup ground cooked pork
¾ cup grated Parmesan
   cheese

1 egg yolk
3 tablespoons dry bread
   crumbs
⅛ teaspoon nutmeg

Brown the sausage meat. Pour off the fat. Add the butter and pork; cook 5 minutes. Cool and mix in the cheese, egg yolk, bread crumbs, and nutmeg. Taste for seasoning.

BEEF-FILLED NOODLES

(Tortellini alla Campagna)

2 cups sifted flour
2 teaspoons salt
3 eggs
2 tablespoons water
1 tablespoon olive oil

1 pound ground beef
½ pound ricotta or cottage
   cheese
¼ teaspoon pepper
⅛ teaspoon nutmeg

Sift the flour and 1 teaspoon salt onto a board. Make a well in the center. Place 2 eggs and the water in the center. Work in the flour gradually, kneading until the dough is smooth and pliable. Add a little flour or water if necessary. Form into a ball, cover with a bowl, and set aside while preparing the filling.

Heat the olive oil in a skillet. Add the beef. Sauté until browned, stirring constantly. Mix with the remaining egg, the ricotta, pepper, nutmeg, and remaining salt. Cool.

Roll out the dough as thin as possible. Cut into 2-inch circles. Place a teaspoonful of the filling on each. Fold over the dough, sealing the edges with the tines of a fork.

Drop into boiling salted water or stock, if available. Cook about 8 minutes, or until they rise to the top. Do not cook too many at once. Drain. Serve with a sauce or melted butter and grated cheese.

Serves 4–6.

GREEN NOODLES
(Lasagne Verdi)

2½ *cups sifted flour*
¼ *teaspoon salt*
2 *eggs, beaten*

¾ *cup puréed cooked*
spinach

Sift the flour and salt onto a board. Make a well in the center and put the eggs and spinach into it. Work in the flour, kneading until a medium-soft dough is formed. (This dough will require a good deal of kneading until it is pliable.) Let stand 10 minutes. Divide the dough in half and roll out as thin as possible. Spread the dough on a cloth and allow to dry about 1½ hours. Roll up the dough as for a jelly roll, but as tight as possible. Cut into 1-inch strips.

Drop into boiling salted water and cook 15 minutes. Drain well. Serve with Tomato or Meat Sauce and grated cheese. *Serves 4.*

GREEN NOODLES, BOLOGNA STYLE
(Lasagne Verdi alla Bolognese)

BOLOGNESE SAUCE

6 *tablespoons butter*
1 *cup finely chopped*
minced onions
½ *cup grated carrots*
1 *pound ground beef*
1 *8-ounce can tomato*
sauce

4 *cups beef broth or*
water
1½ *teaspoons salt*
½ *teaspoon freshly ground*
black pepper
1 *cup heavy cream*

Melt the butter in a saucepan; sauté the onions and carrots 10 minutes. Add the beef; cook, stirring frequently, until no pink remains. Add the tomato sauce, broth, salt, and pepper; cover and cook over low heat 2 hours, stirring occasionally. Mix in the cream and taste for seasoning.

NOODLES

½ *pound spinach*	½ *cup grated Parmesan*
4 *cups sifted flour*	*cheese*
1½ *teaspoons salt*	4 *tablespoons butter*
3 *eggs, beaten*	

Wash and drain the spinach. Cook over low heat 5 minutes. Drain very well. Purée in an electric blender, force through a sieve, or chop very fine. If spinach is wet, cook over low heat until moisture evaporates.

Sift the flour and salt into a bowl. Make a well in the center and put the eggs and spinach into it. Work in the flour with the hands. Turn out onto a floured surface and knead until smooth and elastic. Form into a ball and cover with a bowl; let stand 20 minutes.

Divide dough into 4 pieces and roll out each piece paper-thin, sprinkling with flour as you roll. Let dry 1 hour, then cut into 4-inch squares. Cook a few at a time in boiling salted water 2 minutes. Remove with a slotted spoon and drop into cold salted water. Drain and place on a cloth to dry.

Spread a little sauce in a buttered baking dish. Make as many layers as possible of the noodles, sauce, and grated cheese. End with sauce and cheese. Dot with the butter. Bake in a 375° oven 25 minutes.

Serves 6–8.

HOMEMADE EGG TAGLIATELLE

2 *cups sifted flour*	4 *eggs*
½ *teaspoon salt*	

Sift the flour and salt onto a board. Make a well in the center and place the eggs in it. Work in the flour, kneading until a stiff dough is formed. Add a little more flour if necessary. Cover and let stand 15 minutes. Roll out as thin as possible, and cut into strips like shoe string.

Drop the *tagliatelle* into boiling salted water. Cook 8–10 minutes. Drain well. Serve with butter or with any sauce.

Makes about ½ pound.

CORN-MEAL DUMPLINGS

(Gnocchi alla Romana)

½ cup white corn meal	½ teaspoon white pepper
2 cups water	1 cup grated Parmesan
1½ teaspoons salt	cheese
1 cup milk, scalded	1 cup heavy cream

Mix the corn meal with ½ cup of the water until smooth. Bring the remaining water and the salt to a boil in the top of a double boiler over direct heat. Gradually add the corn meal, stirring constantly until mixture boils. Add the milk, stirring constantly. Place over hot water and cook 30 minutes.

Pour into a wet square or oblong pan to a depth of ½ inch. Chill until firm. Cut into 2-inch oblong or diamond-shaped pieces.

In a buttered baking dish, arrange as many layers as possible of the *gnocchi*, sprinkled with pepper and the Parmesan cheese. Pour the cream over the top. Bake in a 350° oven 40 minutes.

Serves 4–6.

CHEESE DUMPLINGS
(Gnocchi au Gratin)

2 cups milk	1½ cups grated Parmesan
¼ pound butter	cheese
¼ teaspoon salt	4 tablespoons melted
¼ teaspoon nutmeg	butter
2¼ cups sifted flour	1½ cups grated Gruyère or
6 eggs	Swiss cheese

Combine the milk, butter, salt, and nutmeg in a saucepan. Bring to a boil and remove from heat. Add the flour, mixing well. Return to low heat and cook, beating constantly until mixture is smooth and butter begins to ooze. Remove from heat. Add one egg at a time, beating until it is absorbed. Add the Parmesan cheese. Beat well. Let stand 10 minutes.

Shape the mixture into 2-inch sausage-like rolls between lightly floured hands. Drop into boiling salted water. Cook until *gnocchi* rise to the top, about 5 minutes. Drain well. Place in a buttered baking dish. Sprinkle with melted butter and Gruyère cheese.

Bake in a 350° oven 20 minutes.

Serves 6–8.

GREEN GNOCCHI

8 potatoes (2½ pounds)	2 tablespoons grated
cooked and mashed	Parmesan cheese
1½ cups puréed cooked	2 egg yolks, beaten
spinach	1 teaspoon salt
⅓ cup sifted flour	

Beat together the potatoes, spinach, flour, cheese, egg yolks, and salt until light and smooth.

Form into cylinders ½ inch thick and 2 inches long on a lightly floured board. Form one as a test; if it doesn't hold together while cooking, add a little more flour.

Carefully drop into boiling salted water. Don't crowd the pan. Boil until they rise to the surface, about 5 minutes. Drain well.

Serve with Tomato Sauce and grated cheese, or melted butter and cheese.

Serves 6–8.

STUFFED NOODLE PANCAKES

(Cannelloni)

Egg-Noodle Dough (*see recipe*)
1 *cup cooked spinach*
1 *cup ricotta cheese*
2 *tablespoons melted butter*

½ *cup grated Parmesan cheese*
½ *cup Tomato Sauce (see recipe)*

Roll the Egg-Noodle Dough into 2 paper-thin sheets; sprinkle heavily with flour. Cut each sheet into rectangles, 3 by 4 inches, and let dry 1 hour. Cook in boiling salted water 5 minutes. Drain, dip into cold water, drain again, and spread on a towel to dry.

Purée the spinach in an electric blender or chop very fine. Mix with the ricotta cheese, butter, and ¼ cup of the Parmesan cheese. Spread a heaping tablespoonful on each piece of cooked dough and roll up like a jelly roll.

Spread half the Tomato Sauce in a shallow baking dish. Arrange the *cannelloni* over it; cover with the remaining sauce and sprinkle with the remaining Parmesan cheese. Bake in a 450° oven 10 minutes.

Serves 6.

CHEESE MANICOTTI

4 cups sifted flour   ½ pound ricotta cheese
½ teaspoon salt   1½ cups Tomato Sauce
3 eggs, beaten   (see recipe)
1 tablespoon melted butter   Grated Parmesan cheese
¾ cup warm water

Sift the flour and salt onto a board. Make a well in the center; into it put the eggs, butter, and water. Work in the flour gradually, kneading until a soft, smooth dough is formed. Add a little more warm water if the dough is too stiff. Cover and let stand 20 minutes.

Roll out the dough as thin as possible, and cut into pieces about 5 by 7 inches. Spread about 2 tablespoonfuls of the ricotta cheese on each piece and roll up like a jelly roll. Moisten the edges with water and seal the edges and the ends.

Drop carefully into boiling salted water. Boil 10 minutes. Remove carefully with a slotted spoon and drain. Place the *manicotti* in a buttered baking dish, side by side, or use individual dishes. Cover with Tomato Sauce.

Bake in a 400° oven 10 minutes. Serve with grated Parmesan cheese.

Serves 4–6.

CAPPELLETTI WITH BEEF FILLING

2 *cups sifted flour*	½ *pound ricotta cheese or*
2 *teaspoons salt*	*cottage cheese*
3 *eggs*	¼ *teaspoon pepper*
2 *tablespoons water*	⅛ *teaspoon nutmeg*
1 *tablespoon olive oil*	1 *cup grated Parmesan*
1 *pound ground beef*	*cheese*

Sift the flour and 1 teaspoon salt onto a board. Make a well in the center and place 2 eggs and the water into it. Work in the flour gradually, kneading until the dough is smooth and pliable. Add a little more flour or water, if necessary, to make a dough. Set aside while preparing the filling.

Heat the olive oil in a skillet; sauté the beef until browned, stirring constantly. Mix with the ricotta, pepper, nutmeg, and remaining salt. Cool.

Roll out the dough as thin as possible. Cut into 2-inch circles. Place a teaspoon of the filling on each. Fold the dough over, sealing the edges with a fork.

Drop into deep boiling water. Cook about 8 minutes, or until *cappelletti* rise to the surface. Don't crowd the pan. Drain. Serve with the grated cheese.

Serves 4–6.

RAVIOLI

EGG PASTA

2 *cups sifted flour*	½ *teaspoon salt*
2 *eggs*	2 *tablespoons cold water*

Sift the flour onto a board; make a well in the center. In it place the eggs, salt, and water. Work in the flour until a ball of dough is formed. If too dry, add a little more cold water. Scrape the board clean and sprinkle with flour. Knead the dough until very smooth and elastic. Cover with a bowl and let rest 15 minutes while preparing the filling.

FILLING

1 cup ground cooked beef or chicken	¼ teaspoon freshly ground black pepper
¼ cup finely chopped ham	½ teaspoon salt
1 egg, beaten	¼ cup grated Parmesan cheese
¼ teaspoon minced garlic	

Mix together all the ingredients.

Divide the dough in half. Roll out each half paper-thin. Lift dough and sprinkle board and rolling pin with flour when necessary to keep dough from sticking. Cut into strips 2 inches wide. On half of the strips, place a teaspoonful of filling at 2-inch intervals. Cover with remaining strips of dough. Using the index finger, press gently around each mound. Cut into squares with a pastry wheel or knife. Be sure the edges are sealed. Let dry 1 hour.

Cook in deep boiling salted water about 7 minutes, or until they rise to the surface. Drain and serve with melted butter and grated Parmesan cheese or with Tomato Sauce.

Makes about 30.

EGG AND SPINACH RAVIOLI

(Torta Pascualina)

2 cups sifted flour	¾ teaspoon freshly ground black pepper
3 egg yolks	
⅓ cup olive oil	¼ teaspoon nutmeg
½ cup lukewarm water	¼ cup grated Parmesan cheese
2 cups cooked spinach, drained	
	6 eggs
	2 teaspoons salt

Sift the flour onto a board; make a well in the center. Put the egg yolks and 3 tablespoons of the olive oil into it. Gradually work in the flour, adding enough lukewarm water to make a stiff dough. Knead the dough until smooth and elastic. Form into a ball; cover with a cloth and set aside for 10 minutes. Roll out the dough as thin as possible on a lightly floured surface and brush with some of the oil. Cut the dough into 4 pieces, each large enough to fit an oblong baking dish measuring about 8 by 15 inches. Grease the dish and place 2 layers of dough on the bottom.

Mix together the spinach, pepper, nutmeg, and cheese; spread evenly over the dough. With a spoon, make 6 evenly spaced depressions in the spinach mixture. Break an egg into each depression and sprinkle with the salt. Cover with the remaining 2 layers of dough, sealing the edges carefully. Run a pastry wheel or the handle of a knife over the dough, to divide it into 6 equal portions with an egg in each. Brush with oil.

Bake in a 375° oven for 35 minutes, or until lightly browned on top. Serve hot or cold.

Serves 6.

RAVIOLI, NEAPOLITAN STYLE

1½ *cups sifted flour*	¼ *cup dry bread crumbs*
1½ *teaspoons salt*	2 *tablespoons chopped*
1 *egg*	*parsley*
2 *tablespoons warm water*	1 *egg yolk*
¼ *pound ground beef*	3 *tablespoons ice water*
½ *cup cooked chopped*	½ *teaspoon freshly ground*
spinach	*black pepper*

Sift the flour and ½ teaspoon of the salt onto a board; make a well in the center. Place the egg and warm water in it. Work in the flour, kneading until the dough is smooth and elastic. Cover and set aside for 30 minutes.

Mix together the beef, spinach, bread crumbs, parsley, egg yolk, ice water, pepper, and remaining salt.

Roll out the dough as thin as possible. Cut into 3-inch squares. Place 1 teaspoonful of the meat mixture on each. Fold over into a triangle and press the edges together carefully.

Drop into boiling salted water or broth, if available. Boil 15 minutes. Drain.

Serve with Tomato Sauce or with butter and Parmesan cheese. *Serves 4–6.*

RAVIOLI WITH CHEESE

2 cups sifted flour	1 pound ricotta cheese
6 egg yolks	1 cup grated Parmesan
¾ teaspoon salt	cheese
½ cup warm water	2 tablespoons grated onion
(approximately)	1 egg white

Sift the flour onto a board. Make a well in the center. Place 3 egg yolks into it. Add ¼ teaspoon salt and 3 tablespoons water. Work in the flour and knead until a stiff dough is formed, adding more water if necessary. Knead until smooth and elastic. Cover the dough with a bowl and let stand 15 minutes. Divide the dough in half and roll out one half as thin as possible.

Mix together the ricotta cheese, Parmesan cheese, onion, and remaining egg yolks and salt. Place teaspoonfuls of the mixture 2 inches apart on the dough. Roll out remaining dough and place over the cheese. Press the two layers of dough together around each mound of cheese and the edges. Cut the squares apart with a pastry wheel; moisten edges with egg white.

Carefully drop into boiling salted water and boil 10 minutes. Don't crowd the pan. Drain. Serve with melted butter and grated Parmesan cheese or with Tomato Sauce and grated cheese. *Serves 6–8.*

CHINESE NOODLES

2 cups flour   1 cup water
¼ teaspoon salt

Mix the flour, salt, and water until a dough is formed. Turn out onto a floured surface and knead until smooth and elastic. Cover with a damp cloth and let stand 30 minutes.

Knead again, then roll out and stretch very thin. Fold over into 5 layers and slice very thin. Shake to separate the strips and let dry 30 minutes. Cook in deep boiling water 7 minutes, or until tender. Drain. Use as directed in recipes.

Makes ½ pound.

WATER-FRIED NOODLES, CHINESE STYLE
(Mee)

NOODLES

2½ cups sifted flour   2 tablespoons water
3 eggs   Vegetable oil for deep-fat
½ teaspoon baking soda   frying

Sift the flour onto a board. Make a well in the center and into it put the eggs and the baking soda dissolved in the water. Work in the flour, kneading until a stiff dough is formed. Roll into a long strip; fold over and again roll into a strip, repeating at least 10 times. Roll out again, and then fold the dough back and forth into 4-inch strips, with as many folds as possible. With a sharp knife, shred the dough as thin as possible, like very thin noodles, and shake apart.

Heat the fat in a deep saucepan to 380°. At the same time, prepare a large saucepan of boiling water. Drop the noodles into the water and boil 2 minutes. Drain well. Drop the boiled noodles into the fat and fry 3 minutes. Drain well. Drop into the boiling water again and boil 2 minutes. Drain. Place on a platter and keep warm.

CHICKEN MIXTURE

2 *tablespoons vegetable oil*	¼ *cup sliced mushrooms*
¾ *cup chopped onions*	1 *tablespoon soy sauce*
2 *whole chicken breasts,*	
boned and cut into	
cubes	

Heat the oil in a skillet. Sauté the onions 3 minutes. Add the chicken cubes and sauté 10 minutes, stirring frequently. Add the mushrooms, soy sauce, and 2 tablespoons water. Cook 5 minutes, stirring occasionally. Pour over the *mee* (noodles) and serve hot.

Serves 4.

CHINESE EGG-NOODLE DOUGH

6 *eggs*	2 *cups sifted flour*
¼ *teaspoon salt*	(*approximately*)

Beat the eggs. Add the salt and flour, using just enough flour to make a soft dough, but firm enough to roll. Form into a ball; cover with a cloth and let stand 10 minutes. On a floured board, roll out the dough as thin as possible. Let dry 45 minutes. Roll up loosely. Cut into very thin strips. Let dry 4 or 5 hours.

Cook in boiling salted water 5 minutes, or until tender.

These noodles may be kept uncooked for several days in a covered jar, if desired.

Makes about ½ pound.

CHINESE FRIED DUMPLINGS
(Chiao-Tzu)

½ *pound raw pork*
¼ *pound raw shrimp,*
   shelled and deveined
½ *cup lard or oil*
⅓ *cup finely chopped onions*
1 *teaspoon finely chopped*
   ginger root or pow-
   dered ginger
3 *tablespoons soy sauce*

½ *teaspoon sugar*
1 *teaspoon salt*
2 *cups flour*
1 *egg*
⅔ *cup lukewarm water*
½ *cup cold water*
Mustard
Chinese duck sauce

Grind the pork and shrimp. Heat 2 tablespoons lard or oil in a skillet; sauté the onions and ginger 3 minutes. Add the pork and shrimp mixture and sauté 5 minutes, stirring frequently. Blend in the soy sauce, sugar, and salt. Cool.

Sift the flour into a bowl. Make a well in the center and put the egg and warm water into it. Work in the flour. Knead until smooth and elastic. Cover with a bowl and let stand 20 minutes. Roll out paper-thin and cut into 3-inch circles. Put 2 teaspoonfuls of the filling on each and fold over, sealing the edges well.

Heat the remaining lard or oil in a skillet. Arrange the dumplings in it in rows. Fry until lightly browned on bottom. Add the cold water. Cover and cook over low heat 10 minutes. Serve hot with mustard and Chinese duck sauce.

Makes about 32.

CZECHOSLOVAKIAN POTATO NOODLES

2 *pounds potatoes*
3 *cups water*
2 *teaspoons salt*

2 *tablespoons flour*
3 *eggs*
4 *tablespoons butter*

Cook the unpeeled potatoes in boiling water until tender. Drain and peel immediately. Mash very smooth. Add the salt, flour, and eggs. Mix well and knead into a dough. If the mixture is too thin to roll, add a very little additional flour. On a lightly floured board, roll as thin as possible. Roll up loosely. Cut into strips about ¼ inch wide.

Arrange layers of the strips of dough in a buttered baking dish in a crisscross pattern. Dot the top with pieces of the butter.

Bake in a 375° oven 30 minutes, or until browned on top. Serve with poultry or meat dishes.

Serves 4–6.

Classic Spaghetti Dishes

THE classic spaghetti dishes are all native to Italy. It is believed that Spaghetti alla Papalina was devised for one of the Popes who was always seeking a new type of spaghetti preparation. The recipes in this section make excellent first courses. In order to appreciate their unusual flavor, they should not accompany any other dish. These classic spaghetti dishes deserve their reputation and acclaim. Anyone may develop a reputation as a skilled cook by preparing these dishes.

SPAGHETTI WITH WHITE CLAM SAUCE

(Spaghetti alla Vongole, Bianco)

2 quarts small hard-shelled
    clams
½ cup olive oil
¾ cup finely chopped
    onions
2 cloves garlic, minced

¼ teaspoon freshly ground
    black pepper
⅓ cup minced parsley
1 pound spaghetti, cooked
    and drained

Scrub the clams; wash under cold running water until water runs clean. Put in a saucepan; cover and cook over high heat until shells open, shaking the pan frequently. Remove the clams from the shells and strain the juice. Discard any clams that do not open.

Heat the oil in a saucepan; sauté the onions 5 minutes. Add the garlic; sauté 5 minutes. Add the steamed clams, juice, pepper,

and parsley; cook 1 minute. Spoon over the spaghetti. (No cheese is served with this dish.)
Serves 4–6.

SPAGHETTI WITH RED CLAM SAUCE

(Spaghetti alla Vongole, Rosso)

⅓ cup olive oil	2 quarts small hard-shelled
1 cup chopped onions	clams
3 cloves garlic, minced	¼ cup finely chopped
3 cups chopped tomatoes	parsley
1½ teaspoons salt	1 pound spaghetti, cooked
½ teaspoon freshly ground	and drained
black pepper	

Heat the oil in a saucepan; sauté the onions 10 minutes. Add the garlic, tomatoes, salt, and pepper. Cook over low heat 45 minutes. Purée half the sauce in an electric blender or force through a sieve. Return to the saucepan. Taste for seasoning.

Scrub the clams and wash under cold running water until water runs clean. Put in a pan; cover and cook over high heat until shells open; shake the pan frequently. Remove the clams from the shells and strain the juice. Discard any clams that do not open. Add the clams, juice, and parsley to the tomato sauce. Heat. Spoon over the spaghetti. (No cheese is served with this dish.)
Serves 4–6.

SPAGHETTINI WITH OIL, GARLIC, AND PARSLEY

(Spaghettini Aglio e Olio)

½ cup olive oil	1 pound spaghettini (thin
4 whole cloves garlic	spaghetti), cooked and
	drained
	¼ cup minced parsley

Heat the oil in a skillet; brown the garlic in it and discard. Pour the oil over the hot drained spaghettini; sprinkle with the parsley and toss lightly.

Serves 4.

THIN SPAGHETTI WITH OIL AND ANCHOVIES

(Vermicelli con Olio e Acciughe)

½ *cup olive oil*
3 *cloves garlic, minced*
1 *can anchovies, drained and minced*

1 *pound vermicelli or fine noodles, cooked and drained*

Heat the oil in a skillet; sauté the garlic 2 minutes. Mix in the anchovies. Pour over the hot vermicelli and toss lightly.

Serves 4–6.

THIN SPAGHETTI WITH MUSHROOMS AND ANCHOVIES

(Spaghettini alla Campagnola)

¼ *cup olive oil*
6 *anchovy fillets, minced*
2 *cloves garlic, minced*
¼ *pound mushrooms, sliced*
¾ *cup dry white wine*
⅛ *teaspoon dried crushed red peppers*

1 *pound tomatoes, peeled and chopped*
1 *pound spaghettini, cooked and drained*
3 *tablespoons minced parsley*

Heat the oil in a saucepan; sauté the anchovies and garlic 2 minutes. Add the mushrooms; cook 2 minutes. Mix in the wine; cook over high heat 2 minutes. Add the peppers and tomatoes. Cook over low heat 20 minutes. Taste for seasoning. Pour over the spaghettini and sprinkle with the parsley.

Serves 4.

NOODLES WITH EGG-HAM SAUCE

(Fettuccine alla Papalina)

¼ *pound butter*
½ *cup chopped onions*
¼ *pound prosciutto or
  cooked ham, cut
  julienne*
½ *cup sliced, sautéed mushrooms*

4 *egg yolks*
4 *tablespoons freshly grated
  Parmesan cheese*
1 *pound* fettuccine (*see
  recipe*) *or broad egg
  noodles, cooked and
  drained*

Melt 2 tablespoons butter in a skillet; sauté the onions and ham 5 minutes. Stir in the sautéed mushrooms; season to taste.

Beat the egg yolks in the top of a double boiler. Stir in the cheese and the remaining butter, cut into small pieces. Place over hot (not boiling) water and stir constantly with a wooden spoon until thickened.

Put the drained *fettuccine* in a hot bowl; pour the egg mixture over it and toss very well. Sprinkle the ham mixture on the top.
Serves 4.

SPAGHETTI WITH EGG-CREAM SAUCE

(Spaghetti alla Papalina)

8 *egg yolks*
½ *cup heavy cream*
¼ *pound butter, cut into
  small pieces*
1 *teaspoon salt*

1½ *teaspoon pepper*
½ *cup grated Parmesan
  cheese*
1½ *pounds spaghetti,
  cooked and
  drained*

Beat the egg yolks in a saucepan. Add the cream, butter, salt, pepper, and cheese. Mix well. Add the spaghetti, tossing lightly over very low heat until butter melts and spaghetti is well coated.

Serves 6–8.

SPAGHETTI WITH BACON SAUCE

(Spaghetti all'Amatriciana)

¼ *pound bacon, diced*
4 *tablespoons butter*
1 *pound tomatoes, peeled and chopped*
¾ *cup dry white wine*

½ *teaspoon salt*
⅛ *teaspoon dried crushed red peppers*
1 *pound spaghetti, cooked and drained*

Cook the bacon in a saucepan until lightly browned but not crisp. Pour off almost all the fat. Add the butter, tomatoes, wine, salt, and peppers; bring to a boil and cook over low heat 25 minutes. Taste for seasoning and pour over the spaghetti.

Serves 4.

SPAGHETTI WITH BACON-EGG SAUCE

(Spaghetti alla Carbonara)

3 *slices bacon, cut julienne*
4 *tablespoons olive oil*
2 *tablespoons butter*
1 *cup julienne-cut prosciutto ham*

4 *tablespoons grated Parmesan cheese*
2 *eggs, beaten*
1 *pound spaghetti, cooked and drained*

In a skillet, brown the bacon lightly; pour off the fat. Add the oil, butter, and ham. Sauté 5 minutes, but do not let the ingredients brown. Remove from the heat and stir in the cheese, then the eggs. Pour quickly over the hot spaghetti and mix thoroughly.

Serves 4–6.

SPAGHETTI, HOME STYLE
(Spaghetti alla Casalinga)

¼ *pound bacon, chopped*
1 *cup chopped onions*
1 *clove garlic, minced*
1 *stalk celery, chopped*
1 *carrot, grated*
4 *tablespoons tomato paste*
1½ *cups water*

¼ *teaspoon freshly ground black pepper*
½ *teaspoon sugar*
2 *tablespoons chopped parsley*
2 *tablespoons butter*
1 *pound spaghetti, cooked and drained*

Fry the bacon in a saucepan 2 minutes. Mix in the onions, garlic, celery, and carrot. Cook over low heat 10 minutes, stirring frequently. Mix in the tomato paste, water, pepper, and sugar. Cook over low heat 45 minutes, stirring occasionally. Taste for seasoning. Stir in the parsley and butter.

Heap the spaghetti on a hot platter. Pour the sauce over it and toss lightly. Serve immediately.

Serves 4–6.

SPAGHETTI WITH TRUFFLE PUREE

½ *pound butter*
1-*ounce can purée of truffles (available at food specialty shops)*

1 *pound spaghetti, cooked and drained*
1 *cup grated Parmesan cheese*
½ *cup heavy cream*

Melt half the butter in a skillet. Mix in the truffle purée; cook over low heat 5 minutes, but do not let it brown.

Combine the spaghetti, Parmesan cheese, heavy cream, and remaining butter in a large saucepan. Keep over low heat, tossing the spaghetti, until the butter melts. Add the truffle purée. Cover saucepan, remove from heat, and let stand 5 minutes before serving.

Serves 4.

SPAGHETTI WITH TRUFFLE SAUCE
(Spaghetti al Tartufata)

1 can anchovy fillets
¼ cup olive oil
4 tablespoons butter
3 cloves garlic, split
3 tablespoons tomato
    paste
1¾ cups water

¼ teaspoon freshly ground
    black pepper
4 or more truffles, cut
    julienne
1 pound spaghetti,
    cooked and drained

Drain and rinse the anchovies under cold water. Drain again and chop fine. Heat the oil and butter in a saucepan; sauté the garlic 3 minutes, then discard. With a wooden spoon, mix in the anchovies. Stir in the tomato paste mixed with the water and pepper. Bring to a boil and cook over low heat 20 minutes. Add the truffles; taste for seasoning.

Heap the drained spaghetti in a heated deep serving dish. Pour the sauce over it and toss lightly.

Serves 4–6.

MACARONI, LIVORNESE STYLE
(Maccheroni alla Livornese)

4 tablespoons butter
1½ pounds tomatoes,
    chopped
2 teaspoons salt
½ teaspoon pepper
1 pound mushrooms
2 tablespoons flour

2 cups milk
1 pound macaroni, cooked
    and drained
½ cup grated Parmesan
    cheese
¼ pound mozzarella cheese,
    sliced

Melt half the butter in a skillet. Add the tomatoes. Cook over low heat 15 minutes, stirring frequently. Season with 1 teaspoon salt and ¼ teaspoon pepper.

Melt the remaining butter in a saucepan. Sauté the mushrooms 2 minutes, then sprinkle with the flour, stirring until smooth. Add the milk, stirring constantly to the boiling point. Cook over low heat 5 minutes. Add the remaining salt and pepper.

Spread half the macaroni in a buttered baking dish. Cover with the tomatoes and then the mushroom mixture. Add the remaining macaroni. Sprinkle the Parmesan cheese over it. Arrange mozzarella cheese on top. Bake in a 375° oven 30 minutes.

Serves 4–6.

SPAGHETTI WITH FRESH TOMATO SAUCE

(Spaghetti alla Marinara)

¼ *cup olive oil*
2 *cloves garlic, split*
1½ *pounds tomatoes,*
   peeled and diced
1¼ *teaspoons salt*
½ *teaspoon freshly ground*
   black pepper

3 *tablespoons minced*
   parsley
1 *pound spaghetti, cooked*
   and drained
Grated Parmesan cheese

Heat the oil in a saucepan; brown the garlic, then discard. Add the tomatoes, salt, and pepper; cook over low heat 20 minutes, or until liquid is almost evaporated. Taste for seasoning. Mix in the parsley. Pour over the hot spaghetti and serve with grated cheese.

Serves 4–6.

VERMICELLI WITH SPICY TOMATO SAUCE

(Vermicelli con Salsa di Pizzaiola)

¼ cup olive oil
2 cloves garlic, minced
1 29-ounce can tomatoes
1 teaspoon salt
¼ teaspoon dried ground
   red peppers

1 teaspoon orégano
2 tablespoons chopped
   parsley
1 pound vermicelli, cooked
   and drained

Heat the olive oil in a saucepan; sauté the garlic 3 minutes. Mix in the tomatoes, salt, peppers, and orégano. Cook over high heat 15 minutes, stirring frequently. Add the parsley.

Heap the vermicelli on a hot platter and pour the sauce over it. *Serves 4–6.*

SPAGHETTI WITH BAGNA CAUDA SAUCE

¼ pound butter
¼ cup olive oil
6 cloves garlic, minced
8 anchovies, minced

1 (or more) truffle, sliced
   thin
1 pound spaghetti, cooked
   and drained

Combine the butter, olive oil, and garlic in the top of a double boiler. Place over hot water and cook over low heat, stirring constantly, until the butter melts. Remove the double boiler from the heat, but leave the top part over the hot water.

Stir in the anchovies and truffle. Cover and let stand 10 minutes. Pour the sauce over the spaghetti and serve. *Serves 4.*

NOODLES WITH WALNUT SAUCE

(Noodles alla Graneresi)

1 *clove garlic, minced*	2 *teaspoons salt*
1 *cup ground walnuts*	½ *teaspoon pepper*
1 *pound ricotta cheese*	1 *pound broad noodles,*
1 *cup grated Parmesan*	*cooked and drained*
cheese	

Pound or roll the garlic and walnuts together until a paste is formed. Place in a bowl with the ricotta and Parmesan cheese, salt, and pepper. Add the hot noodles. Toss lightly with two forks until noodles are coated with the nut mixture.

Serves 4–6.

SPAGHETTI WITH SPICED MEAT BALLS

(Polpette con Spaghetti)

1 *pound chopped beef*	2 *tablespoons olive oil*
½ *cup chopped onions*	1 *clove garlic, minced*
½ *cup soft bread crumbs*	1 *8-ounce can tomato sauce*
3 *tablespoons ketchup*	1 *cup water*
2 *eggs, lightly beaten*	1 *cup chopped celery*
Dash cinnamon	1 *pound thin spaghetti,*
Dash ground cloves	*cooked and drained*
Dash nutmeg	½ *cup grated Parmesan*
¾ *teaspoon salt*	*cheese*
¼ *teaspoon pepper*	

Mix together the beef, onions, bread crumbs, ketchup, eggs, cinnamon, cloves, nutmeg, salt, and pepper. Shape into 1-inch balls. Heat the oil in a skillet; brown the meat balls and garlic. Add the tomato sauce, water, and celery; cook over low heat 15 minutes.

Pour the meat balls and sauce over the spaghetti, and sprinkle with grated Parmesan cheese.

Serves 4.

GREEN NOODLES WITH MEAT SAUCE

(Lasagne Verdi alla Bolognese)

¼ *pound butter*	½ *cup dry white wine*
2 *tablespoons olive oil*	3 *tablespoons tomato*
½ *cup chopped onions*	*sauce*
½ *pound ground beef*	½ *cup water*
1½ *teaspoons salt*	1 *pound green noodles,*
½ *teaspoon freshly ground*	*cooked and drained*
black pepper	

Heat the butter and oil in a saucepan; sauté the onions 10 minutes. Mix in the meat and cook until browned. Add the salt, pepper, wine, and tomato sauce. Cook over low heat 1 hour, adding water from time to time.

In a buttered casserole or baking dish, arrange successive layers of the noodles and sauce, starting with the noodles and ending with the sauce. Bake in a 375° oven 15 minutes.

Serves 4–6.

EGG NOODLES WITH MEAT SAUCE
(Tagliatelle al Ragu)

4 tablespoons butter
¾ cup chopped onions
¼ cup chopped celery
½ cup grated carrots
¼ pound prosciutto or
    cooked ham, cut
    julienne
¾ pound ground beef
2 tablespoons tomato paste
¾ cup dry red wine

1½ cups water
1 teaspoon salt
½ teaspoon freshly ground
    black pepper
Egg-Noodle Dough (see
    recipe) or 1 pound
    medium egg noodles,
    cooked and drained
Grated Parmesan cheese

Melt the butter in a saucepan; sauté the onions, celery, carrots, and ham 10 minutes, stirring frequently. Add the beef; cook 20 minutes, stirring frequently. Mix the tomato paste with the wine and add to the saucepan with the water, salt, and pepper. Cover and cook over low heat 45 minutes. Mix occasionally. Taste for seasoning. Pour over the hot noodles and serve with grated cheese.
Serves 4.

EGG NOODLES WITH BUTTER AND CHEESE
(Fettuccine all'Alfredo)

1 pound Fettuccine (see
    recipe) or broad egg
    noodles

¼ pound butter
1 cup freshly grated Par-
    mesan cheese

This dish is best prepared with homemade *fettuccine*, thinly rolled, but if you don't want to make them, buy *fettuccine* or broad noodles. Cook the noodles in boiling salted water until tender but still firm. Drain.

Cut the butter into small pieces and put in a deep, heated serving dish. Add the *fettuccine* and sprinkle with the cheese. Using a fork and spoon, quickly and lightly toss the *fettuccine* until well coated with the butter and cheese.

Serves 4.

MACARONI IN CREAM

(Maccheroni alla Crema)

4 tablespoons butter	2 cups heavy cream, scalded
1 pound macaroni, cooked and drained	1 cup grated Parmesan cheese

Melt the butter in a saucepan. Remove from the heat. Add the macaroni and toss lightly. Add the cream and mix gently. Toss in the cheese until well blended. Serve immediately.

Serves 4–6.

BROAD NOODLES WITH TOMATO-MEAT SAUCE

(Pappardelle alla Toscana)

This dish is best prepared with homemade noodles. Make Egg Noodle Dough recipe and cut noodles 1½ inches wide or buy the broadest noodles available.

5 dried mushrooms	1 cup dry red wine
4 tablespoons olive oil	1½ cups peeled, chopped
2 tablespoons butter	tomatoes
½ cup chopped onions	1 teaspoon salt
¼ pound prosciutto or cooked ham, cut julienne	½ teaspoon freshly ground black pepper
¼ pound chicken livers, diced	Egg Noodle Dough (see recipe) or 1 pound broad noodles, cooked and
2 teaspoons flour	drained

Wash the dried mushrooms, cover with warm water, and let soak 15 minutes. Drain and slice thin.

Heat the oil and butter in a saucepan; sauté the onions 5 minutes. Add the ham; sauté 5 minutes. Mix in the livers and mushrooms; sauté 3 minutes. Blend in the flour, then stir in the wine; cook over medium heat 5 minutes. Add the tomatoes, salt, and pepper; cook over low heat 25 minutes. Taste for seasoning.

Pour half the sauce over the noodles and toss. Serve the remaining sauce in a bowl.

Serves 4.

LASAGNE WITH SAUSAGE AND TOMATO SAUCE
(Lasagne alla Calabrese)

¼ *pound hot Italian sausages*
¼ *pound sweet Italian sausages*
⅓ *cup olive oil*
2 *cloves garlic, minced*
1 *29-ounce can Italian-style tomatoes, chopped*
1 *6-ounce can tomato paste*
½ *teaspoon basil*
½ *teaspoon salt*
¼ *teaspoon black pepper*
1 *pound mushrooms, sliced*
1 *pound lasagne (broad noodles), cooked and drained*
1 *pound ricotta cheese*
¾ *pound mozzarella cheese, sliced*
¼ *cup grated Parmesan cheese*

Remove the skin of the sausages and chop the meat. Lightly brown the sausage meat in a saucepan. Pour off the fat and add 4 tablespoons of the oil to the saucepan. Stir in the garlic for 1 minute, then add the tomatoes, tomato paste, basil, salt, and pepper. Bring to a boil and cook over low heat 45 minutes, stirring frequently. Taste for seasoning.

Sauté the mushrooms in the remaining oil 5 minutes. In a shallow oiled baking dish, spread a layer of *lasagne*, then layers of ricotta, mozzarella, mushrooms, and sauce. Continue until all the ingredients are used, ending with the sauce. Sprinkle with the Parmesan cheese. Bake in a 400° oven 20 minutes, or until very hot.

Serves 4–6.

SPAGHETTI, TAORMINA STYLE

¾ *pound bacon*
2 *cups finely chopped*
   onions
2 *cloves garlic, minced*
½ *pound mushrooms, sliced*
6 *anchovies, mashed*

½ *cup sliced black olives*
1 *pound spaghetti, cooked*
   and drained
2 *tablespoons olive oil*
½ *cup grated Parmesan*
   cheese

Fry the bacon until crisp. Drain, reserving 2 tablespoons of the fat. Crumble the bacon and reserve. Sauté the onions in the bacon fat 10 minutes, stirring frequently. Remove the onions and set aside. Sauté the garlic and mushrooms in the remaining fat 5 minutes, stirring frequently. Add the anchovies and olives and sauté 5 minutes. Return the onions and bacon.

Put the spaghetti on a hot platter and toss with the olive oil. Pour the onion mixture over the top. Serve with the grated cheese. *Serves 4–6.*

UMBRIAN SPAGHETTI

6 *anchovies*
½ *cup olive oil*
2 *cloves garlic, sliced*
1 *tablespoon tomato paste*
½ *cup water*

½ *teaspoon freshly ground*
   black pepper
2 *truffles (optional)*
1 *pound spaghetti, cooked*
   and drained

Cover the anchovies with water and let soak 10 minutes. Drain well and mash very fine.

Heat the olive oil in a skillet; sauté the garlic until brown. Discard the garlic. Add the anchovies, tomato paste, water, and black pepper to the oil. Mix well together. Cook over low heat 30 minutes. Taste for seasoning. Mix in the truffles. Pour the sauce over the spaghetti, toss lightly, and serve. *Serves 4–6.*

SPAGHETTI WITH OLIVE OIL AND MUSHROOMS
(Spaghetti all'Ostrica)

1 *cup olive oil*
¾ *pound mushrooms, sliced*
1 *teaspoon salt*
1 *teaspoon freshly ground black pepper*

2 *tablespoons chopped parsley*
1 *teaspoon lemon juice*
1 *pound spaghetti, cooked and drained*

Heat ½ cup of the olive oil in a skillet. Add the mushrooms, salt, and ¼ teaspoon of the pepper. Sauté 5 minutes, stirring frequently. Mix in the parsley and lemon juice.

Pour the remaining olive oil and pepper over the spaghetti and toss together lightly. Pour the mushroom mixture over the top and serve immediately.

Serves 4–6.

VERMICELLI NAPOLETANA

2 *tablespoons butter*
½ *cup olive oil*
1 *29-ounce can tomatoes*
2 *tablespoons tomato paste*
1 *bay leaf*
1 *teaspoon basil*
1 *cup water*

1 *teaspoon salt*
½ *teaspoon freshly ground black pepper*
1 *pound vermicelli, cooked and drained*
½ *cup grated Parmesan cheese*

Heat the butter and oil in a skillet. Mix in the tomatoes and tomato paste. Cook over medium heat 5 minutes. Add the bay leaf, basil, water, salt, and pepper. Cook over low heat 25 minutes.

Heap the vermicelli on a hot platter. Pour the sauce over it and sprinkle with the Parmesan cheese.

Serves 4–6.

NOODLES WITH PEAS

(Pasta e Piselli)

2 tablespoons butter
4 slices bacon, diced
1 pound green peas,
    shelled, or 1 package
    frozen, thawed
½ cup chopped onions
1 cup water

½ teaspoon salt
⅛ teaspoon sugar
⅛ teaspoon meat extract
1 cup grated Parmesan
    cheese
1 pound noodles, cooked
    and drained

In a skillet, combine the butter, bacon, peas, onions, and water. Bring to a boil, cover, and cook over low heat 20 minutes, or until peas are very soft and water is almost absorbed. Season with the salt, sugar, and meat extract.

In a heated bowl, toss the cheese with the hot noodles, then with the green pea mixture.

Serves 4–6.

SPAGHETTI, SYRACUSE STYLE

(Spaghetti alla Siracusa)

½ cup olive oil
2 cloves garlic, sliced
3 cups peeled, diced
    tomatoes
1 small eggplant, peeled
    and diced
2 green peppers, sliced
½ cup sliced black olives
    (Italian or Greek, if
    possible)

1 tablespoon capers
1 teaspoon orégano
3 anchovy fillets, minced
½ teaspoon salt
½ teaspoon black pepper
1 pound spaghetti, cooked
    and drained

Heat the oil in a large skillet and brown the garlic slices. Discard garlic. Add the tomatoes and eggplant to the oil and cook over low heat 30 minutes. Add the peppers, olives, capers, orégano, anchovies, salt, and pepper. Cover and cook 10 minutes longer, adding a little water if necessary. Taste for seasoning. Pour over the spaghetti.

Serves 4–6.

SPAGHETTI IN HERB SAUCE

(Spaghetti alla Novelli)

3 tablespoons olive oil
1½ cups chopped onions
8 anchovy fillets, minced
2 tablespoons chopped
  parsley
1 clove garlic, minced
1 stalk celery, chopped
  fine
½ teaspoon rosemary
½ teaspoon sage

1 pound tomatoes, peeled
  and diced
½ cup dry white wine
¾ teaspoon salt
½ teaspoon black pepper
1 pound spaghetti, cooked
  and drained
Grated Parmesan or Romano
  cheese

Heat the oil in a saucepan; sauté the onions 10 minutes. Add the anchovies, parsley, garlic, celery, rosemary, and sage; cook over low heat 5 minutes. Add tomatoes and cook 30 minutes. Mix in the wine, salt, and pepper; cook 1 minute longer. Taste for seasoning.

Pour the sauce over the spaghetti and serve with the grated cheese.

Serves 4.

WIDE NOODLES WITH HERB SAUCE
(Lasagne con Pesto)

8 *fresh basil leaves or* ¾
    teaspoon dried
4 *tablespoons minced*
    parsley
2 *cloves garlic, minced*
1 *cup grated Pecorino or*
    Parmesan cheese

¼ *cup olive oil*
½ *teaspoon freshly ground*
    black pepper
1 *recipe* Lasagne *or* 1
    pound packaged
    lasagne, cooked and
    drained

Try to get fresh basil if possible. If not, soak the dried basil in lukewarm water 5 minutes to freshen. Drain.

In a mortar with pestle or on a board with a sharp knife, pound or chop together the basil, parsley, and garlic until a paste is formed. Add the cheese and oil alternately, a little at a time, pounding all the while. Mix in the pepper. Toss with the hot *lasagne.* Any other *pasta* may be served in the same manner.

Serves 4–6.

NOODLES WITH TOMATOES, CHEESE, AND OLIVES
(Tagliatelle con Olive)

1 *20-ounce can tomatoes*
¼ *pound butter*
¼ *cup olive oil*
¾ *cup chopped onions*
1½ *teaspoons salt*
½ *teaspoon freshly ground*
    black pepper
1 *teaspoon orégano*

Egg-Noodle Dough (*see*
    recipe) *or* 1 *pound*
    medium egg noodles,
    firmly cooked and
    drained
½ *pound mozzarella cheese,*
    cut into ¼-*inch cubes*
¼ *cup grated Parmesan*
    cheese
½ *cup sliced black olives*

Chop the tomatoes fine.

Heat half the butter and all the oil in a saucepan; sauté the onions 5 minutes. Add the tomatoes, salt, and pepper; bring to a boil and cook over high heat 10 minutes. Mix in the orégano.

Melt the remaining butter in a casserole. Add the noodles, mozzarella, and 2 tablespoons of the Parmesan cheese. Toss well. Pour the sauce over the mixture, sprinkle with the remaining Parmesan cheese, and arrange the olives on top. Bake in a 350° oven 15 minutes, or until the cheese melts.

Serves 4–6.

SPAGHETTI, CORSICAN STYLE

1 *pound dried codfish*	2 *tablespoons chopped*
4 *tablespoons butter*	*parsley*
1½ *pounds tomatoes*	2 *tablespoons olive oil*
6 *anchovies, mashed*	½ *teaspoon freshly ground*
¼ *cup ground nuts*	*black pepper*
2 *cloves garlic, minced*	1 *pound spaghetti, cooked*
	and drained

Soak the codfish overnight in water to cover; change the water twice. Drain well. Add fresh water, bring to a boil, and cook 30 minutes. Drain. Flake the fish carefully, removing all the bones.

Melt the butter in a saucepan; cook the tomatoes over low heat 15 minutes, stirring occasionally. Purée in an electric blender or force through a sieve; return to the saucepan. Mix in the anchovies, nuts, garlic, parsley, olive oil, pepper, and codfish. Cook over low heat 30 minutes, adding a little water if the sauce becomes too thick. Taste for seasoning. Pour over the spaghetti and serve.

Serves 4.

With Fish

*F*ISH is a misunderstood and neglected food in the United States and should be served more frequently for a properly balanced diet. It is lower in both calories and fat than meat and, when combined with *pasta*, offers a great many interesting possibilities to menu planning. Almost all the recipes in this section are suitable for meatless days and Lent.

SPAGHETTI WITH SHRIMP

⅓ cup olive oil
1½ cups sliced onions
2 cloves garlic, minced
1 29-ounce can Italian-style tomatoes
1½ teaspoons salt
¼ teaspoon dried ground red peppers

1 teaspoon basil
1 cup cooked or canned green peas
1 pound cooked shrimp, shelled and deveined
1 pound spaghetti, cooked and drained

Heat the olive oil in a saucepan; sauté the onions and garlic 10 minutes, stirring frequently. Add the tomatoes, salt, dried red peppers, and basil. Bring to a boil, cover, and cook over low heat 30 minutes. Add the peas and shrimp. Cook 10 minutes, stirring occasionally. Taste for seasoning.

Heap the spaghetti on a platter. Pour the sauce over it, toss lightly, and serve immediately.

Serves 4–6.

SPAGHETTI WITH SHRIMP SAUCE

1 *pound shrimp*
2 *tablespoons butter*
1 *clove garlic*
¼ *cup chopped celery*
¼ *cup chopped green
    pepper*
2 *tablespoons flour*

¼ *teaspoon salt*
⅛ *teaspoon pepper*
⅛ *teaspoon thyme*
1 *cup milk*
1 *pound spaghetti, cooked
    and drained*
Grated Parmesan cheese

Clean shrimp and cook in boiling, salted water 5 minutes.

Melt the butter in a saucepan. Add the garlic, celery, and green pepper. Sauté 5 minutes. Remove garlic. Remove pan from heat. Blend in the flour, salt, pepper, and thyme. Return to heat and gradually stir in milk. Cook over low heat, stirring frequently, until mixture is smooth and thickened. Stir in shrimp and cook 3 minutes. Pour the sauce over hot spaghetti. Sprinkle with Parmesan cheese.

Serves 4.

SHRIMP AND MUSHROOM CASSEROLE

½ *pound fine noodles,
    cooked and drained*
1 *10½-ounce can mush-
    room soup*
½ *cup milk*
1 *pound shrimp, cooked
    and cleaned*

1 *cup cooked or canned
    green peas*
½ *teaspoon salt*
Dash cayenne pepper
1 *tablespoon grated onion*
½ *cup dry bread crumbs*
¼ *cup melted butter*

Spread half the noodles in a buttered casserole. Mix together the soup and milk until smooth. Add the shrimp, green peas, salt, cayenne pepper, and onion. Taste for seasoning. Pour the mixture over the noodles and cover with the remaining noodles. Sprinkle with the bread crumbs and melted butter. Bake in a 375° oven 30 minutes.

Serves 4–6.

SINGAPORE SHRIMP AND VERMICELLI

(Laksa)

3 *cups chopped onions*
2 *cloves garlic, minced*
¼ *cup ground nuts*
2 *teaspoons salt*
½ *teaspoon dried ground chili peppers*
¼ *teaspoon saffron*
½ *teaspoon grated lemon rind*

2 *teaspoons anchovy paste*
4 *tablespoons oil*
1½ *pounds raw shrimp, shelled and deveined*
½ *cup fine grated coconut*
2 *cups milk*
½ *pound vermicelli or fine noodles, cooked and drained*

Pound together the onions, garlic, nuts, salt, chili peppers, saffron, lemon rind, and anchovy paste.

Heat the oil in a skillet and sauté the mixture 3 minutes, stirring almost constantly. Add the shrimp; mix well and sauté 2 minutes. Add the coconut and milk; bring to a boil and cook over low heat 1 minute. Serve on the vermicelli.

Serves 4–6.

SHRIMP AND MACARONI IN CHILI SAUCE

½ cup olive oil
2½ cups chopped onions
1 clove garlic, minced
2 green peppers, cut
    julienne
3 8-ounce cans tomato
    sauce
1½ teaspoons salt

¼ teaspoon dried ground
    chili peppers
1 teaspoon sugar
1 pound cooked shrimp,
    shelled and deveined
1 pound elbow macaroni,
    cooked and drained
3 hard-cooked eggs,
    quartered

Heat the oil in a saucepan; sauté the onions, garlic, and green peppers 10 minutes. Mix in the tomato sauce, salt, chili peppers, and sugar. Cook over low heat 1 hour, stirring occasionally. Add the shrimp and macaroni. Mix lightly and heat thoroughly. Taste for seasoning. Serve garnished with the eggs.

Serves 4–6.

SPAGHETTI, MEXICAN STYLE

3 tablespoons olive oil
1½ cups chopped onions
1 clove garlic, minced
2 tablespoons flour
2 cups beef broth
2 tomatoes, peeled and
    chopped
1 teaspoon salt
¼ teaspoon pepper
2 teaspoons chili powder
½ pound mushrooms,
    sliced

½ pound shrimp, cooked,
    cleaned, and chopped
1 cup diced cooked
    chicken
1 pound spaghetti, cooked
    and drained
4 tablespoons melted
    butter
1½ cups grated Parmesan
    cheese

Heat the oil in a saucepan; sauté onions and garlic 5 minutes. Blend in the flour. Add the broth gradually, stirring constantly to the boiling point. Mix in tomatoes, salt, pepper, and chili powder. Cook over low heat 15 minutes. Add the mushrooms. Cook 5 minutes. Stir in the shrimp, chicken, and spaghetti.

Spread half the spaghetti mixture in a buttered casserole. Sprinkle with half the butter and cheese. Repeat the layers. Bake in a 375° oven 25 minutes.

Serves 4–6.

LOBSTER AND MACARONI CASSEROLE

¼ pound (1 stick) butter
½ cup grated onion
1 clove garlic, minced
4 tablespoons flour
3 cups chicken broth
3 tablespoons tomato paste
⅓ cup dry white wine
¾ pound cooked lobster meat, diced
¼ cup chopped parsley
1 teaspoon salt
½ teaspoon freshly ground black pepper
1 pound elbow macaroni, cooked and drained
½ cup grated Gruyère or Swiss cheese
1 teaspoon paprika

Melt half the butter in a saucepan; sauté the onion and garlic 5 minutes, stirring frequently. Blend in the flour. Gradually add the broth, stirring constantly to the boiling point. Mix in the tomato paste. Cook over low heat 15 minutes. Add the wine, lobster, parsley, salt, and pepper. Cook over low heat 5 minutes. Add the macaroni and taste for seasoning.

Pour the mixture into a buttered casserole. Sprinkle with the cheese and paprika. Dot with the remaining butter. Bake in a 375° oven 20 minutes, or until lightly browned.

Serves 4–6.

NOODLES WITH LOBSTER SAUCE

¼ *pound (1 stick) butter*
3 *tablespoons grated onion*
⅓ *cup sifted flour*
2 *cups milk*
1 *cup heavy cream*
2 *teaspoons salt*

¼ *teaspoon white pepper*
½ *pound cooked lobster*
 meat, cubed
3 *tablespoons dry sherry*
1 *pound medium noodles,*
 cooked and drained

Melt the butter (reserving 2 tablespoons) in a saucepan. Sauté the onion 3 minutes. Blend in the flour until smooth. Gradually add the milk and cream, stirring constantly to the boiling point. Add the salt and pepper and cook over low heat 5 minutes.

Melt the remaining butter in a skillet. Sauté the lobster meat 5 minutes, stirring occasionally. Add to the sauce. Add the sherry. Cook over low heat 10 minutes.

Arrange the noodles in 6 individual mounds on a large platter. Make a well in the center of each and pour the sauce into the wells. *Serves 6.*

SPAGHETTI WITH RED LOBSTER SAUCE

(Spaghetti Fra Diavalo)

⅓ *cup olive oil*
1 *cup grated onion*
2 *cloves garlic, minced*
1 *29-ounce can Italian-*
 style tomatoes
1½ *teaspoons salt*
¼ *teaspoon dried ground*
 red peppers

1 *teaspoon orégano*
2 *1½-pound live lobsters,*
 split, or 4 African
 lobster tails
2 *tablespoons chopped*
 parsley
1 *pound spaghetti, cooked*
 and drained

Heat ¼ cup olive oil in a saucepan; sauté the onion and garlic 10 minutes. Add the tomatoes, salt, red peppers, and orégano. Cook over low heat 30 minutes.

Remove the meat from the raw lobster or tails and slice. Heat the remaining olive oil in a skillet. Add the lobster meat and sauté 10 minutes. Add to the tomato sauce with the parsley. Cook 10 minutes. Taste for seasoning. Pour over spaghetti.

Serves 4–6.

LOBSTER AND SPAGHETTI CASSEROLE

2 tablespoons butter
1 cup grated Parmesan
  cheese
1 cup grated mozzarella
  cheese

1 pound thin spaghetti,
  cooked and drained
1 cup melted butter
2 cups cubed, cooked
  lobster meat

Rub a casserole with the 2 tablespoons butter.

Combine the Parmesan and mozzarella and dust the casserole with about 2 tablespoons of the cheese mixture.

Spread half the spaghetti in the casserole. Sprinkle with half the melted butter, half the lobster meat, and half the remaining cheese. Repeat the layers of spaghetti, butter, lobster meat and cheese. Bake in a 400° oven 20 minutes.

Serves 4–6.

SPAGHETTI WITH MUSSELS

½ cup olive oil
3 cloves garlic
2 cups canned tomatoes
2 tablespoons tomato paste
1 teaspoon salt
¼ teaspoon dried ground
  red peppers

1 teaspoon orégano
2 tablespoons chopped
  parsley
36 mussels, washed and
  scrubbed
1 pound spaghetti, cooked
  and drained

Heat the olive oil in a saucepan; sauté the garlic until brown. Discard the garlic cloves. Add the tomatoes, tomato paste, salt, red peppers, orégano, and parsley. Cook over low heat 40 minutes.

Place the mussels in a pan and cook over low heat, stirring frequently, until the shells open. Remove the mussels from their shells, reserving ½ cup liquid. Mix the liquid with the tomato mixture.

Arrange the mussels on top of the spaghetti and pour the sauce over them.

Serves 4–6.

OYSTER AND NOODLE CASSEROLE

¼ pound (1 stick) butter	1 cup grated cheddar
4 tablespoons flour	cheese
2 cups milk	½ pound medium noodles,
1 teaspoon salt	cooked and drained
¼ teaspoon freshly ground	24 shucked oysters
black pepper	2 tablespoons lemon juice

Melt the butter in a saucepan. Pour off half of the butter and reserve. Blend the flour into the butter in the saucepan. Gradually add the milk, stirring constantly to the boiling point. Cook over low heat 5 minutes. Mix in the salt, pepper, and cheese until the cheese melts.

Toss the reserved melted butter with the noodles. Spread half the noodles in a buttered casserole. Arrange the oysters over the noodles and sprinkle with the lemon juice. Cover with the remaining noodles. Pour the cheese sauce on top. Bake in a 375° oven 30 minutes.

Serves 4.

MACARONI WITH CLAM-MUSHROOM SAUCE

¼ *pound* (1 *stick*) *butter*
2 *cloves garlic, minced*
¼ *pound mushrooms, sliced*
1 *cup minced parsley*
2 *cups coarsely chopped*
fresh clams or 2 10½-
ounce cans minced
clams, drained

½ *teaspoon salt*
¼ *teaspoon freshly ground*
black pepper
¾ *pound shell or elbow*
macaroni

Melt the butter in a skillet and lightly brown the garlic. Stir in the mushrooms and parsley. Cover and cook over low heat 5 minutes, stirring once or twice. Mix in the clams, salt, and pepper. Cook 5 minutes. Pour over the macaroni.

Serves 3–4.

SPAGHETTI WITH CRAB MEAT

¼ *cup olive oil*
¾ *cup chopped onions*
1 *clove garlic, minced*
1 *green pepper, chopped*
1 *29-ounce can tomatoes*

¼ *teaspoon dried ground*
red peppers
½ *teaspoon basil*
¾ *pound crab meat*
1 *pound spaghetti, cooked*
and drained

Heat the olive oil in a saucepan; sauté the onions, garlic, and green pepper 10 minutes. Mix in the tomatoes, red peppers, and basil. Cook over low heat 30 minutes, stirring frequently. Pick over the crab meat, add, and cook 3 minutes only. Taste for seasoning.

Spread the spaghetti on a hot platter. Pour the crab meat mixture over it and serve immediately.

Serves 4.

FETTUCCINE WITH CRAB MEAT

1 *pound crab meat*
⅜ *pound (1½ sticks)*
   softened butter
½ *cup heavy cream*
½ *cup graded Parmesan*
   cheese

1 *pound fettuccine or egg*
   noodles, cooked and
   drained
½ *teaspoon freshly ground*
   black pepper
Salt

Pick over the crab meat, discarding any cartilage. Place in the top of a double boiler with 2 tablespoons of the butter and let it heat.

Beat the remaining butter with the cream and cheese. Have the drained noodles in a saucepan and add the butter mixture. Toss until noodles are thoroughly coated. Add the pepper, crab meat, and salt to taste. Toss again.

Serves 6.

FISHERMAN'S CRAB MEAT

4 *tablespoons butter*
1 *cup chopped onions*
1 *clove garlic, minced*
¾ *cup chopped celery*
2 *tablespoons chopped*
   parsley
1 *19-ounce can tomatoes*
2 *tablespoons tomato*
   paste

1 *teaspoon salt*
¼ *teaspoon dried ground*
   red peppers
2 *teaspoons chili powder*
1 *pound crab meat*
½ *pound spaghetti, cooked*
   and drained
½ *cup grated cheddar*
   cheese

Melt the butter in a saucepan; sauté the onions, garlic, celery, and parsley 10 minutes. Add the tomatoes, tomato paste, salt, dried red peppers, and chili powder. Cook over low heat 1 hour, stirring occasionally. Mix in the crab meat lightly. Cook 5 minutes, stirring frequently. Fold in the spaghetti. Heat and serve, sprinkled with the grated cheese.

Serves 4–6.

LINGUINI WITH ANCHOVIES

(Linguini al uso Lucania)

½ *cup olive oil*
4 *cloves garlic, minced*
1 *can anchovies, mashed*
½ *teaspoon freshly ground*
    black pepper

12 *black olives, chopped fine*
12 *green olives, chopped fine*
1 *pound* linguini, *cooked*
    and drained

Heat the olive oil in a skillet. Add the garlic and anchovies; cook over low heat until the garlic browns, stirring frequently. Mix in the pepper and black and green olives. Add the *linguini* and toss lightly until well coated with the sauce. Serve immediately.

Serves 4.

SPAGHETTI WITH ONIONS AND ANCHOVIES

½ *cup olive oil*
1½ *pounds onions, chopped*
8 *anchovies, chopped*
1 *8-ounce can tomato*
    sauce

½ *cup dry white wine*
1 *teaspoon orégano*
½ *cup chopped parsley*
1 *pound spaghetti, cooked*
    and drained

Heat the olive oil in a saucepan; sauté the onions 10 minutes, stirring frequently. Mix in the anchovies, tomato sauce, wine, and orégano. Cook over low heat 45 minutes. Add a little water if the sauce is too thick. Add the parsley. Taste for seasoning.

Heap the spaghetti on a platter and pour the sauce over it. Toss lightly and serve immediately.

Serves 4–6.

SWEDISH BAKED FISH AND MACARONI
(Ugnstekt Fisk och Makaroni)

3 *cups water*	½ *teaspoon freshly ground*
½ *cup chopped carrots*	*black pepper*
½ *cup chopped onions*	½ *cup heavy cream*
2 *teaspoons salt*	1 *egg yolk*
2 *pounds white fish or sea*	¼ *cup dry white wine*
bass	½ *pound elbow macaroni,*
2 *tablespoons butter*	*cooked and drained*
2 *tablespoons flour*	¼ *cup grated Swiss cheese*
1 *teaspoon salt*	3 *tablespoons dry bread*
	crumbs

Bring the water to a boil; add the carrots, onions, salt, and fish. Cover and cook over low heat 15 minutes. Drain. Reserve 1½ cups stock. Remove skin and bones and cut fish into 2-inch pieces.

Melt the butter in a saucepan; blend in the flour, salt, and pepper. Add fish stock and cream, stirring steadily until sauce thickens. Beat the egg yolk in a bowl. Add the hot sauce, stirring steadily to prevent curdling. Mix in the wine. In a 2-quart buttered baking dish, spread a layer of macaroni and sprinkle with some grated cheese; add a layer of fish and then a layer of sauce. Repeat until all ingredients are used up, ending with a layer of macaroni. Sprinkle with bread crumbs and bake in a 400° oven 20 minutes.

Serves 6.

NOODLE-STUFFED FISH

¼ pound (1 stick) butter
1 cup chopped onions
1 clove garlic, minced
2 tablespoons chopped
    parsley
3 teaspoons salt
1 teaspoon freshly ground
    black pepper

1 pimiento, chopped
½ pound medium noodles,
    cooked and drained
1 egg, beaten
1 4-pound fish (sea bass,
    trout, or white fish),
    split for stuffing

Melt half of the butter in a skillet; sauté the onions and garlic 10 minutes, stirring occasionally. Mix in the parsley, 1 teaspoon of the salt, ¼ teaspoon of the pepper, the pimiento, and the noodles. Stir in the beaten egg.

Rub the fish with the remaining salt and pepper. Stuff with the noodle mixture. Place in a buttered baking dish and dot with the remaining butter. Bake in a 350° oven 40 minutes, basting occasionally with the liquid in the dish.

Serves 4–6.

SPAGHETTI WITH TUNA

(Spaghetti al Tonno)

¼ cup olive oil
½ cup chopped onions
1 clove garlic, minced
1 cup chopped celery
3 8-ounce cans tomato
    sauce
1¼ teaspoons salt
½ teaspoon black pepper
¼ teaspoon crushed dried
    red peppers

1 teaspoon basil
2 7¾-ounce cans tuna fish,
    drained and broken
    into chunks
¼ cup capers, drained
1 can anchovies, minced
½ cup sliced Italian olives
1 pound spaghetti, cooked
    and drained

Heat the oil in a saucepan; sauté the onions 10 minutes. Mix in the garlic, celery, tomato sauce, salt, black pepper, red peppers, and basil. Bring to a boil and cook over low heat 30 minutes. Add the tuna fish, capers, anchovies, and olives. Cook 5 minutes longer. Pour over the hot spaghetti.

Serves 4–6.

SPAGHETTI WITH RED TUNA SAUCE

2 tablespoons olive oil
1 7¾-ounce can tuna fish,
    flaked
1 clove garlic, minced
2 tablespoons parsley
1 29-ounce can tomatoes
2 tablespoons tomato paste

½ teaspoon salt
¼ teaspoon dried ground
    red peppers
1 teaspoon orégano
1 pound spaghetti, cooked
    and drained

Heat the olive oil in a saucepan. Add the tuna fish, garlic, and parsley; sauté 10 minutes, stirring frequently. Add the tomatoes, tomato paste, salt, and dried peppers. Cook over low heat 1½ hours, stirring occasionally. Stir in the orégano and cook 5 minutes longer.

Place the spaghetti on a hot platter and pour the sauce over it. Toss lightly and serve.

Serves 4.

SPAGHETTI WITH SAVORY TUNA SAUCE

4 tablespoons butter
2 onions, chopped
1 clove garlic, chopped
2 7¾-ounce cans tuna fish, flaked
½ teaspoon salt

¼ teaspoon pepper
2 cups chili sauce
2 tablespoons chopped parsley
1 pound spaghetti, cooked and drained

Melt the butter in a skillet; sauté the onions and garlic 10 minutes. Add tuna fish; cook over medium heat until lightly browned. Mix in the salt, pepper, chili sauce, and parsley. Cook over low heat 5 minutes. Taste for seasoning.

Heap the spaghetti on a hot platter and pour sauce over it.

Serves 4–6.

OREGON CASSEROLE

6 tablespoons butter
½ cup chopped onions
2 tablespoons flour
1 cup milk
1 teaspoon salt
¼ teaspoon freshly ground black pepper
½ pound broad noodles, cooked and drained

2 cups cooked or canned green peas
6 hard-cooked eggs, halved
1 7¾-ounce can tuna fish, drained and flaked
½ cup grated Parmesan cheese
1 teaspoon paprika

Melt half the butter in a saucepan; sauté the onions 5 minutes, stirring frequently. Blend in the flour. Gradually add the milk, stirring constantly to the boiling point. Cook over low heat 5 minutes. Season with the salt and pepper.

Spread half the noodles in a buttered casserole. Arrange layers of the green peas, eggs, and tuna fish, followed by half the sauce. Cover with the remaining noodles and sauce. Sprinkle with the cheese and paprika. Dot with the remaining butter. Bake in a 350° oven 30 minutes.

Serves 4–6.

BAKED SPAGHETTI WITH FISH SAUCE

(Tallarines Chalacos)

1 *cup olive or vegetable oil*	2 *teaspoons salt*
1½ *cups finely chopped onions*	½ *teaspoon dried ground chili peppers*
1 *cup chopped red or green peppers*	1 *pound spaghetti, cooked and drained*
1 *pound fillet of sole, snapper, or other white-meat fish, cut into bite-sized pieces*	½ *cup grated Parmesan cheese*
	2 *tablespoons butter*

Heat half the oil in a skillet; sauté the onions and peppers 10 minutes; add the remaining oil. Add the fish, salt, and chili peppers. Cook over low heat 10 minutes, stirring frequently. Taste for seasoning.

Spread the spaghetti in a buttered casserole, cover with the fish mixture, sprinkle with the cheese, and dot with the butter. Bake in a 400° oven 15 minutes.

Serves 4.

SMOKED SALMON CASSEROLE

3 tablespoons olive oil
¾ cup chopped onions
1 clove garlic, minced
1 29-ounce can tomatoes
1½ teaspoons salt
½ teaspoon freshly ground
    black pepper
1 bay leaf
½ teaspoon basil
3 tablespoons butter

¼ pound mushrooms,
    thinly sliced
3 egg yolks
½ pound smoked salmon,
    thinly sliced and cut
    into small pieces
½ pound spaghetti,
    cooked and drained
3 tablespoons bread crumbs
½ cup beef broth

Heat the oil in a saucepan; sauté the onions and garlic 10 minutes, stirring frequently. Add the tomatoes, salt, pepper, bay leaf, and basil. Cook over low heat 1½ hours, stirring frequently.

Melt the butter in a skillet; add the mushrooms. Sauté until browned, stirring frequently.

Beat the egg yolks in a bowl. Gradually add ¾ of the tomato sauce, beating constantly to prevent curdling. Add the mushrooms, salmon, and spaghetti and mix together lightly.

Dust a buttered casserole with the bread crumbs. Pour the spaghetti mixture into it. Bake in a 350° oven 20 minutes.

Combine the broth and the remaining tomato sauce. Heat and taste for seasoning. Serve in a sauceboat.

Serves 3–4.

SALMON ORIENTALE

2 salmon steaks, cut 1 inch
  thick
2 teaspoons salt
¼ teaspoon pepper
¼ cup flour
4 tablespoons butter
2 cups sliced onions
1 cup chopped green
  pepper
3 stalks celery, chopped
2 tablespoons cornstarch
2 cups chicken broth
1 cup cooked or canned corn
  kernels
2 tablespoons soy sauce
1 teaspoon sugar
1 pound spaghetti, cooked
  and drained

Cut the salmon into 2-inch cubes, discarding the skin and bones. Dip the cubes in a mixture of the salt, pepper, and flour, coating all sides. Melt the butter in a skillet. Add salmon and brown lightly on all sides. Remove salmon. In the butter remaining, sauté the onions, green pepper, and celery 10 minutes. Mix cornstarch and broth until smooth. Add to skillet, stirring constantly to the boiling point, then cook over low heat 5 minutes. Add the corn, soy sauce, and sugar. Cook 1 minute. Taste for seasoning.

Spread the spaghetti in a buttered casserole and arrange the salmon over it. Pour sauce over all. Cover the casserole. Bake in a 350° oven 30 minutes, removing the cover for the last 5 minutes. *Serves 4–6.*

SALMON AND NOODLES, ALASKAN STYLE

3 onions, sliced
2 carrots, diced
2 cups water
3 teaspoons salt
½ teaspoon freshly ground
 black pepper
3 salmon steaks, cut in
 half

4 tablespoons butter
4 tablespoons flour
1 cup milk
1 teaspoon paprika
½ pound medium noodles,
 cooked and drained
2 tablespoons chopped
 parsley

Combine the onions, carrots, and water in a saucepan. Sprinkle
2 teaspoons of the salt and ¼ teaspoon of the pepper on the
salmon and arrange over the vegetables. Cover and bring to a boil,
then cook over low heat 25 minutes, or until the fish is tender.
Remove the fish carefully and keep warm. Strain the stock and
reserve 1 cup.

Melt the butter in a saucepan; blend in the flour. Gradually add
the milk, stirring constantly to the boiling point. Add the reserved
stock, the remaining salt and pepper, and the paprika. Cook over
low heat 5 minutes. Add the noodles and parsley. Mix lightly.

Arrange the noodle mixture on a hot serving platter or individual
plates. Place the salmon on top and serve.

Serves 4–6.

CHINESE FRIED NOODLES

5 *dried mushrooms*
½ *cup hot water*
½ *cup peanut or vegetable*
    oil
½ *cup sliced bamboo shoots*
1 *cup shredded cabbage*
    (*Chinese, if possible*)
2 *teaspoons salt*
1 *tablespoon cornstarch*
2 *tablespoons soy sauce*

1 *tablespoon dry sherry*
1 *tablespoon grated ginger*
    root or 1 teaspoon
    powdered ginger
½ *pound uncooked shrimp,*
    shelled and deveined
½ *pound fine noodles,*
    cooked, drained, and
    chilled 3 hours

Soak the mushrooms in the hot water 10 minutes. Drain and slice.

Heat 3 tablespoons of the oil in a skillet. Add the bamboo shoots and mushrooms; sauté 3 minutes. Add the cabbage and 1 teaspoon of the salt. Cook 5 minutes, stirring frequently. Remove from heat and set aside.

Mix the cornstarch, soy sauce, sherry, and ginger until smooth. Pour over the shrimp. Heat 2 tablespoons of the oil in a skillet and add the undrained shrimp. Cook 6 minutes, stirring frequently. Add the cabbage mixture and cook 1 minute, stirring frequently.

Heat the remaining oil in a skillet. Add the chilled noodles and remaining salt. Fry 5 minutes, turning the noodles frequently. Add the shrimp mixture and fry 2 minutes longer.

Serves 4–6.

THAI NOODLES WITH SEAFOOD AND PORK

1 *pound Chinese vermi-
    celli or fine egg
    noodles*
1¼ *cups oil*
¼ *pound raw pork, diced*
½ *pound raw shrimp,
    shelled, deveined,
    and diced*
¼ *pound crab meat*
1 *tablespoon soy sauce*
1 *tablespoon vinegar*

2 *teaspoons anchovy
    paste*
1 *tablespoon sugar*
1½ *teaspoons salt*
4 *eggs, beaten*
1 *cup bean sprouts*
3 *tablespoons chopped
    chives or green onions*
¼ *teaspoon ground
    coriander*

Break the vermicelli into small pieces and drop into boiling salted water. Cook 1 minute and drain well. Spread on a flat surface to dry. Heat 1 cup oil in a skillet; fry the vermicelli until crisp. Drain.

Heat the remaining oil in a skillet; sauté the pork 10 minutes. Add the shrimp, crab meat, soy sauce, vinegar, anchovy paste, sugar, and salt; cook over low heat 5 minutes. Stir in the eggs until set. Mix in the bean sprouts and vermicelli; cook 5 minutes. Turn out onto a platter; sprinkle with the chives and coriander.

Serves 6–8.

With Meat

M EAT is the foundation of America's diet and a favorite with most people. Unfortunately, it is also expensive. *Pasta* helps to stretch the servings, and in many cases one-dish meals are possible, simplifying cooking and serving. Recipes from many countries are included, offering a wide variety of unusual preparations.

BEEF-ALMOND CASSEROLE

½ cup olive oil	½ teaspoon basil
1 cup thinly sliced onions	1 cup slivered almonds
1 clove garlic, minced	3 eggs
1½ pounds ground beef	½ cup grated Parmesan
2 tomatoes, peeled and	cheese
chopped	1 pound spaghetti, broken
½ cup dry red wine	in half, cooked, and
2½ teaspoons salt	drained
¼ teaspoon freshly ground	2 egg yolks
black pepper	½ cup heavy cream

Heat the olive oil in a skillet; sauté the onions and garlic 10 minutes, stirring frequently. Add the beef. Sauté 10 minutes, stirring frequently. Mix in the tomatoes, wine, 1½ teaspoons of the salt, the pepper and basil. Cook 10 minutes. Stir in the almonds.

Beat the eggs in a bowl. Mix in the cheese and spaghetti lightly. Spread half the mixture in a buttered casserole, with the meat mixture over it. Cover with the remaining spaghetti mixture.

Beat together the egg yolks, cream, and remaining salt and pour over the top. Bake in a 350° oven 25 minutes, or until set and lightly browned.

Serves 4–6.

STEAK AND MACARONI CASSEROLE

2 *pounds steak*
3 *teaspoons salt*
1 *teaspoon freshly ground*
   black pepper
1 *cup grated cheddar*
   cheese

1 *cup dry bread crumbs*
2 *eggs, beaten*
Vegetable oil for deep-fat
   frying
4 *cups cooked macaroni*

Cut the steak into 1-inch squares. Sprinkle with 1½ teaspoons of the salt and ½ teaspoon of the pepper. Dip the steak pieces into ½ cup of the cheese, then into the bread crumbs, the eggs, and once again into the bread crumbs. Heat the oil to 375°. Drop several pieces of the meat into the fat at a time and fry 1 minute. Drain.

Spread the macaroni in a buttered casserole. Sprinkle with the remaining salt, pepper, and cheese. Arrange the steak pieces on top. Bake in a 450° oven 10 minutes, or until browned on top. Serve with broiled tomatoes, if desired.

Serves 4–6.

NOODLE CASSEROLE, SOUTHERN STYLE

4 tablespoons butter
1 cup chopped onions
1 clove garlic, minced
1 green pepper, chopped
2 10½-ounce cans
    tomato soup
1 cup water
2 tablespoons tomato
    paste
½ pound mushrooms, sliced

1½ cups cooked or canned
    corn kernels
2 tablespoons salad oil
2 pounds ground beef
1½ teaspoons salt
½ teaspoon freshly ground
    black pepper
1 pound broad noodles,
    cooked and drained
1 cup grated American
    cheese

Melt the butter in a saucepan; sauté the onions, garlic, and green pepper 10 minutes, stirring frequently. Mix in the soup, water, tomato paste, mushrooms, and corn kernels. Cook over low heat 15 minutes.

Heat the oil in a skillet. Add the beef and cook over high heat, stirring constantly, until the meat is brown. Season with the salt and pepper. Combine the meat with the sauce and cook over low heat 5 minutes. Taste for seasoning.

Spread half the noodles in a buttered casserole. Cover with half the meat mixture and half the cheese. Repeat the layers. Bake in a 375° oven 20 minutes.

Serves 6–8.

GREEK MACARONI CASSEROLE

(Pastichio)

3 *tablespoons olive oil*
1 *cup chopped onions*
1 *pound ground beef*
¾ *cup peeled, chopped*
   tomatoes
1½ *teaspoons salt*
½ *teaspoon freshly ground*
   black pepper

¼ *teaspoon orégano*
½ *cup grated Parmesan*
   cheese
1 *pound short-cut (or*
   elbow) macaroni,
   cooked and drained

Heat the oil in a skillet; cook the onions and meat over high heat, stirring steadily, for 5 minutes. Mix in the tomatoes, salt, pepper, and orégano; cook over low heat 5 minutes. Mix in the cheese. Taste for seasoning.

In a buttered 2-quart casserole, spread half the macaroni. Spread the meat mixture over it and cover with the remaining macaroni. Prepare the sauce:

2 *tablespoons butter*
1 *tablespoon flour*
½ *teaspoon salt*
⅛ *teaspoon white pepper*

1 *cup milk*
1 *egg yolk*
¼ *cup grated Parmesan*
   cheese

Melt the butter in a saucepan; blend in the flour, salt, and pepper. Add the milk gradually, stirring steadily to the boiling point. Cook over low heat 5 minutes. Beat the egg yolk and cheese in a bowl; add the hot sauce slowly, stirring steadily to prevent curdling. Pour over the macaroni. Bake in a 375° oven 30 minutes, or until browned.

Serves 4–6.

ITALIAN SPAGHETTI CASSEROLE

3 tablespoons olive oil
½ cup chopped onions
1 pound ground beef
¼ pound mushrooms,
    sliced
½ cup green peppers, cut
    julienne
1½ teaspoons salt
¼ teaspoon freshly ground
    black pepper

½ teaspoon orégano
2 tablespoons minced
    parsley
2 cans spaghetti sauce
1 pound spaghetti, cooked
    and drained
¾ cup grated Parmesan
    cheese

Heat the oil in a skillet; sauté the onions 10 minutes. Add the meat; cook over medium heat until browned, stirring frequently. Mix in the mushrooms, green peppers, salt, pepper, orégano, parsley, and half the spaghetti sauce. Cook over low heat 5 minutes. Mix the spaghetti with the remaining sauce.

Spread half the spaghetti in a greased casserole; sprinkle with half the cheese. Spread half the meat mixture over it. Repeat layers with remaining ingredients. Cover casserole and bake in a 375° oven 30 minutes; remove the cover for the last 10 minutes.

Serves 4–6.

CHILI-MACARONI CASSEROLE

2 tablespoons olive oil
1 cup thinly sliced onions
½ cup chopped green
    peppers
1 pound ground beef
1 16-ounce can chili beans

1 29-ounce can tomatoes
1¼ teaspoons salt
1 tablespoon chili powder
1½ cups macaroni, half
    cooked and drained

Heat the oil in a skillet; sauté the onions and green peppers 10 minutes. Add the meat; cook over medium heat, stirring almost steadily, until no pink remains. Turn into a greased casserole with the beans, tomatoes, salt, chili powder, and macaroni. Mix well; cover and cook over low heat 30 minutes.

Serves 4–6.

NOODLE CASSEROLE

2 tablespoons butter	¾ teaspoon salt
1 cup chopped onions	¼ teaspoon freshly ground
1 green pepper, chopped	black pepper
1½ pounds ground lean beef	¾ pound medium egg noodles, cooked and
2 tablespoons tomato paste	drained
1 tablespoon A.1. Sauce	½ pound thinly sliced American cheese

Melt the butter in a saucepan; sauté the onions 5 minutes. Add the green pepper; sauté 5 minutes. Mix in the beef until lightly browned. Blend in the tomato paste, A.1. Sauce, salt, and pepper. Cover and cook over low heat 25 minutes.

In a 2-quart buttered casserole, make successive layers of the noodles, cheese, and meat mixture, starting with the noodles and ending with the cheese. Bake in a 350° oven 15 minutes, or until cheese melts and is bubbly hot. Serve with garlic bread and green salad.

Serves 4–6.

HAMBURGER-NOODLE CASSEROLE

2 tablespoons vegetable
  oil
¾ cup chopped onions
1½ pounds ground beef
1 10¾-ounce can con-
  densed tomato soup
1 10½-ounce can beef
  broth

4 ounces uncooked fine
  noodles
2 cups canned green peas
1 cup sliced mushrooms
½ teaspoon freshly ground
  black pepper
1 cup grated cheddar
  cheese

Heat the oil in a skillet; sauté the onions 5 minutes. Add the
beef; cook over medium heat, stirring almost steadily, until
browned. Mix in the tomato soup, broth, and noodles. Cook over
low heat 10 minutes. Turn into a casserole; mix in the peas, mushrooms, and pepper and add salt to taste. Sprinkle with the cheese.
Bake in a 375° oven 30 minutes.
Serves 4–6.

BAKED SPAGHETTI AND MEAT CASSEROLE

½ cup olive oil
1 cup finely chopped
  onions
1 pound ground beef
¼ cup slivered almonds
1 29-ounce can tomatoes
1½ teaspoons salt

½ teaspoon freshly ground
  black pepper
¼ teaspoon orégano
1 pound spaghetti, cooked
  and drained
⅓ cup grated Parmesan
  cheese

Heat the oil in a saucepan; sauté the onions 5 minutes. Mix in
the meat until browned. Add the nuts, tomatoes, salt, pepper, and
orégano. Cover and cook over low heat 30 minutes. Taste for seasoning and mix in the spaghetti. Turn into a buttered casserole;
sprinkle with the cheese. Bake in a 350° oven 25 minutes, or until
very hot and cheese is melted.
Serves 4–6.

CHINESE BEEF AND NOODLES

(Gnow Low Mein)

½ *pound fine noodles*	1 *cup bean sprouts*
3 *tablespoons oil*	1 *tablespoon sugar*
1 *pound ground beef*	1 *cup beef broth*
1 *teaspoon salt*	2 *teaspoons cornstarch*
½ *teaspoon pepper*	2 *tablespoons water*
1 *clove garlic, minced*	¼ *cup sliced green onions*

Cook the noodles according to directions on the package. Drain and rinse under cold water. Drain well and chill.

Heat the oil in deep skillet; brown the meat, stirring frequently to prevent lumps from forming. Add the salt, pepper, garlic, bean sprouts, sugar, and broth. Bring to a boil. Mix together the cornstarch and water; stir into the skillet until mixture thickens. Mix in the noodles and heat. Sprinkle with the green onions.

Serves 4–6.

JAPANESE BEEF AND NOODLES

(Sukiyaki)

2 *pounds sirloin steak*	1 *cup sliced celery*
4 *tablespoons sesame or*	1 *cup sliced bamboo shoots*
vegetable oil	½ *pound mushrooms, sliced*
½ *cup beef broth*	*thin*
¾ *cup soy sauce*	1 *cup shredded spinach*
¼ *cup sugar*	4 *green onions, sliced*
1 *tablespoon dry sherry*	1 *pound vermicelli,*
2 *cups thinly sliced onions*	*cooked and drained*

Have the steak cut paper-thin into pieces about 2 inches by 3 inches.

Heat the oil in a large skillet. Add the meat and brown on both sides. Combine the broth, soy sauce, sugar, and sherry in a bowl. Add half of this mixture to the meat. Push the meat to one side of the skillet. Add the onions and celery; cook over low heat 3 minutes. Add the remaining soy mixture, the bamboo shoots, mushrooms, and spinach. Cook over low heat 3 minutes. Add the green onions and cook 1 minute. Heap the vermicelli on one side of a platter and the sukiyaki on the other and serve immediately.

This dish is particularly suited for preparation at the table in a chafing dish.

Serves 4–6.

SWISS SPAGHETTI AND BEEF

4 tablespoons butter
½ cup chopped onions
1 green pepper, chopped
1 pound ground beef
1 19-ounce can tomatoes
1½ teaspoons salt
½ teaspoon pepper

¾ pound Gruyère or Swiss cheese, cubed
1 pound spaghetti, cooked and drained
½ cup grated Gruyère or Swiss cheese

Melt the butter in a saucepan. Sauté the onions and green pepper 5 minutes. Add the beef; cook over high heat, stirring constantly until browned. Add the tomatoes, salt, and pepper. Cook over low heat 1 hour. Mix in the cubed cheese; cook 5 minutes. Add the spaghetti and mix well. Serve with a bowl of the grated cheese.

Serves 4.

BEEF AND MACARONI HASH

3 tablespoons butter
1 cup chopped onions
1 clove garlic, minced
2 green peppers, chopped
3 tomatoes, chopped
2 tablespoons flour
1 cup beef broth or water

1½ teaspoons salt
¼ teaspoon freshly ground
    black pepper
2 cups cooked, diced beef
½ pound elbow macaroni,
    half cooked and
    drained

Melt the butter in a skillet; sauté the onions, garlic, green peppers, and tomatoes 10 minutes, stirring frequently. Mix the flour with the broth or water and add, stirring constantly to the boiling point. Cook over low heat 5 minutes. Add the salt, pepper, beef, and macaroni. Cook over low heat 15 minutes. Taste for seasoning.
Serves 4.

MOCK TAMALE PIE

2 cups boiling water
1 pound medium noodles
3 tablespoons butter
½ cup chopped onions
1 pound ground beef
1 19-ounce can tomatoes
1 cup water
1 cup cooked or canned
    corn kernels

1 cup cooked or canned
    green peas
2 teaspoons salt
1 tablespoon chili powder
½ cup sliced black olives
1 cup grated cheddar
    cheese

Pour boiling water over the noodles. Let soak for 10 minutes; drain.

Melt the butter in a large skillet. Sauté the onion and ground beef 5 minutes, stirring frequently. Mix in the tomatoes, water, corn, peas, salt, chili powder, black olives, cheese, and noodles. Pour into a buttered casserole. Bake in a 350° oven 45 minutes. *Serves 4–6.*

MACARONI GOULASH

3 tablespoons butter	2 teaspoons paprika
¼ cup chopped onion	2 cups chopped or canned
¼ cup chopped green	tomatoes
pepper	1 pound elbow macaroni,
1 pound ground beef	cooked and drained
1¼ teaspoons salt	½ cup sour cream
½ teaspoon freshly ground	
black pepper	

Melt the butter in a deep skillet; sauté the onion and green pepper 5 minutes. Add the beef; cook over medium heat until browned, stirring almost constantly. Mix in the salt, pepper, paprika, and tomatoes; cover and cook over low heat 20 minutes. Add the macaroni; cook 5 minutes. Mix in the sour cream; taste for seasoning.
Serves 4–6.

BEEF STEW WITH MACARONI

3 tablespoons olive oil	1 bay leaf
1 cup chopped onions	½ teaspoon rosemary
2 pounds beef, cut into	1½ pounds tomatoes,
1-inch cubes	peeled and chopped
2 teaspoons salt	½ pound elbow macaroni,
¼ teaspoon freshly ground	half cooked and
black pepper	drained

Heat the olive oil in a heavy saucepan or Dutch oven; brown the onions and beef. Add the salt, pepper, bay leaf, rosemary, and tomatoes. Cover and cook over low heat 1¼ hours, or until the beef is tender. Mix in the macaroni and a little water if the sauce is too thick. Cook 5 minutes. Discard the bay leaf. Taste for seasoning.

Serves 4–6.

CHIPPED BEEF AND NOODLES

4 tablespoons butter
½ cup grated onions
½ pound dried chipped
    beef, shredded
6 eggs
4 tablespoons cream cheese
½ cup cottage cheese

2 tablespoons chopped
    parsley
1 teaspoon salt
¼ teaspoon freshly ground
    black pepper
½ pound fine noodles,
    cooked and drained

Melt the butter in a skillet; sauté the onions and chipped beef 10 minutes, stirring frequently. Transfer the mixture to the top of a large double boiler and place over hot water.

Beat the eggs in a bowl. Mix the cream cheese and cottage cheese together until smooth and add to the eggs with the parsley, salt, pepper, and noodles. Mix well. Add to the chipped-beef mixture. Stir constantly until the eggs are set.

Serves 4–6.

BEEF AND PRUNES WITH SPAGHETTI

½ cup olive oil
1 cup chopped onions
2 cloves garlic, minced
1 pound beef, cut into
    ½-inch cubes
2 8-ounce cans tomato
    sauce
¾ cup dry red wine

½ teaspoon salt
½ teaspoon nutmeg
12 prunes, presoaked and
    pitted
1 pound spaghetti, cooked
    and drained
½ cup grated Parmesan
    cheese

Heat the olive oil in a saucepan; sauté the onions, garlic, and beef until browned, stirring frequently. Add the tomato sauce, wine, salt, and nutmeg. Cook over low heat 40 minutes. Add the prunes. Cook 30 minutes. Correct seasoning if necessary.

Heap the spaghetti on a platter and pour the sauce over it. Serve with the cheese.

Serves 4–6.

MEAT BALLS WITH SPAGHETTI

1 *pound ground beef*	¼ *cup olive oil*
½ *cup grated onion*	½ *cup chopped celery*
1 *clove garlic, minced*	1½ *cups tomato sauce*
2 *eggs*	⅛ *teaspoon dried ground*
¼ *cup bread crumbs*	*red peppers*
1½ *teaspoons salt*	1 *pound spaghetti,*
¼ *teaspoon freshly ground*	*cooked and drained*
black pepper	

Mix together the beef, onion, garlic, eggs, bread crumbs, 1 teaspoon salt, and the pepper until well blended. Shape into 1-inch balls. Heat the olive oil in a skillet and brown the meat balls. Add the celery, tomato sauce, red peppers, and remaining salt. Cook over low heat 20 minutes.

Heap the spaghetti on a hot platter and pour the sauce over it.

Serves 4.

SPAGHETTI WITH STEAK SAUCE

½ cup olive oil
1 cup chopped onions
2 pounds steak, cut into
    small cubes
½ pound mushrooms, sliced
2 tablespoons chopped
    parsley
1 clove garlic, minced
1 6-ounce can tomato paste
1 8-ounce can tomato
    sauce

2 tomatoes, peeled and
    cubed
2 teaspoons salt
¾ teaspoon freshly ground
    black pepper
½ teaspoon basil
1½ pounds spaghetti,
    cooked and drained
½ cup melted butter
¾ cup grated Parmesan
    cheese

Heat the oil in a skillet; sauté the onions and cubed steak. Mix in the mushrooms; sauté 5 minutes. Add the parsley, garlic, tomato paste, tomato sauce, tomatoes, salt, pepper, and basil. Cook over very low heat 2 hours. Taste for seasoning.

Heap the spaghetti on a hot platter; toss with the butter. Pour the sauce in the center and sprinkle with the Parmesan cheese. *Serves 6–8.*

MACARONI WITH SWEET SAUCE

(Maccheroni con Salsa Dolce)

3 tablespoons olive oil
1 cup chopped onions
2 cloves garlic, minced
1 pound ground beef
1 16-ounce can tomatoes,
    drained and chopped

1½ teaspoons salt
½ teaspoon black pepper
1 pound ricotta cheese
3 tablespoons honey
1 pound elbow macaroni,
    cooked and drained

Heat the oil in a saucepan; sauté the onions 10 minutes. Mix in the garlic and beef; cook until browned, stirring frequently. Add the tomatoes, salt, and pepper. Cook over low heat 45 minutes. Mix in the ricotta and honey. Heat and pour over the hot macaroni. *Serves 6–8.*

SPAGHETTI WITH MIXED MEAT SAUCE

2 tablespoons olive oil
½ pound ground beef
½ pound ground pork
¾ cup chopped onions
1 clove garlic, minced
1 29-ounce can tomatoes
1 6-ounce can tomato paste
2 bay leaves
1 teaspoon basil

1½ teaspoons salt
¼ teaspoon dried ground
  red peppers
2 tablespoons chopped
  parsley
2 tablespoons melted
  butter
1 pound spaghetti,
  cooked and drained

Heat the olive oil in a saucepan. Mix in the beef, pork, onions, and garlic. Cook over high heat, stirring constantly, until the meat is browned. Add the tomatoes, tomato paste, bay leaves, basil, salt, and red peppers. Cover and cook over low heat 1½ hours, adding water if the sauce becomes too thick. Taste for seasoning. Stir in the parsley and melted butter.

Pour the sauce over the spaghetti and serve immediately. *Serves 4–6.*

NOODLES WITH STROGANOFF SAUCE

4 tablespoons butter
¼ cup chopped green onions
1 clove garlic, minced
½ pound mushrooms, sliced
1 pound ground beef
2 tablespoons lemon juice
¼ cup dry red wine
1 cup beef broth
1 teaspoon salt

¼ teaspoon freshly ground
   black pepper
½ pound medium noodles,
   half cooked and
   drained
1 cup sour cream
3 tablespoons chopped
   parsley

Melt the butter in a large skillet; sauté the green onions, garlic, and mushrooms 5 minutes. Add the beef; cook over medium heat, stirring almost constantly, until meat is browned. Mix in the lemon juice, wine, broth, salt, and pepper. Bring to a boil and cook over low heat 15 minutes. Add the half-cooked noodles; cover and cook 5 minutes. Blend in the sour cream, taste for seasoning, and heat, but do not let boil. Sprinkle with the parsley.

Serves 4.

MACARONI WITH STUFFED ARTICHOKES

(Maccheroni con Carciofi)

6 artichokes
¼ pound ground beef
¼ pound ground pork
¼ cup minced parsley
3 tablespoons grated
   Parmesan cheese
¼ cup pine nuts or sliced
   almonds
1¾ teaspoons salt

½ teaspoon pepper
4 tablespoons olive oil
2 cups chopped onions
1 29-ounce can Italian-
   style tomato sauce
1 clove garlic, minced
1 pound macaroni, cooked
   and drained

Cut the sharp tips off the artichokes with scissors. Cover artichokes with water; bring to a boil and cook 10 minutes. Drain.

Press artichoke leaves open in a downward direction on a hard surface, then cut out the chokes (furry centers). Stand artichokes upright and stuff centers with a mixture of the beef, pork, parsley, cheese, nuts, ¾ teaspoon salt, and ¼ teaspoon pepper.

Heat the oil in a saucepan; sauté the onions 10 minutes. Add the tomato sauce, garlic, and the remaining salt and pepper. Bring to a boil and cook over low heat 10 minutes. Arrange the artichokes in the sauce in an upright position. Cover and cook over low heat 45 minutes. Carefully transfer the artichokes to a serving dish. Pour the sauce over the macaroni. The artichokes are eaten at the same time. Grated cheese may be served with the macaroni too.

Serves 6.

STUFFED PASTA

2 tablespoons butter
¾ cup chopped onions
1 clove garlic, minced
1 pound ground beef
1½ teaspoons salt
¼ teaspoon freshly ground black pepper
¼ teaspoon orégano
2 eggs, beaten
¼ cup coarsely chopped almonds
½ pound ricotta or cottage cheese

1 cup grated mozzarella cheese
¾ cup grated Parmesan cheese
1 pound ziti, cannelloni, rigatoni, or tufoli, cooked and drained
3 cups Tomato Sauce (see recipe)
¾ pound mozzarella cheese, thinly sliced
¼ cup melted butter

Melt the butter in a skillet; sauté the onions and garlic 5 minutes. Add the meat; cook over high heat, stirring frequently until browned. Remove from heat; mix in the salt, pepper, orégano, eggs, nuts, ricotta cheese, mozzarella cheese, and ¼ cup of the Parmesan. Mix thoroughly.

Stuff the *pasta*, using a teaspoon or demitasse spoon, depending upon the size of the tube.

Spread 1 cup of the Tomato Sauce in a shallow baking dish. Arrange half the tubes over it, a layer of Tomato Sauce, then a layer of sliced mozzarella cheese, sprinkled with half the remaining Parmesan cheese. Repeat the sequence and sprinkle with the melted butter. Bake in a 375° oven 35 minutes.

Serves 8–10.

LASAGNE, BOLOGNA STYLE

¼ *pound salt pork,*
  chopped
½ *pound ground beef*
½ *pound ground pork*
½ *pound ground veal*
1½ *cups chopped onions*
1 *carrot, grated*
2 *cups beef broth*
2 *teaspoons tomato paste*
1 *teaspoon salt*

¼ *teaspoon pepper*
½ *pound mushrooms*
¼ *pound chicken livers,*
  coarsely chopped
½ *cup heavy cream*
1 *pound lasagne*
½ *pound ricotta cheese*
1 *cup grated Parmesan*
  cheese

Cook the salt pork in a saucepan until there are at least 2 tablespoons of fat. Add beef, pork, veal, onions, and carrot. Brown well, stirring constantly. Mix in the broth, tomato paste, salt, and pepper. Cover and cook over low heat 1 hour. Add the mushrooms, livers, and cream. Cook 15 minutes longer. Taste for seasoning.

In a buttered baking dish, arrange as many layers as possible of the *lasagne*, ricotta cheese, sauce, and Parmesan cheese, ending with the sauce and Parmesan cheese. Bake in a 375° oven 20 minutes.

Serves 4–6.

MEAT-MACARONI LOAF

1 *pound ground beef*
2 *eggs, beaten*
½ *cup water*
1½ *teaspoons salt*
¼ *teaspoon freshly
    ground black pepper*

2 *tablespoons chopped
    parsley*
¼ *pound macaroni, cooked,
    drained, and chopped*
½ *cup grated Parmesan
    cheese*
2 *tablespoons olive oil*

Mix together the meat, eggs, water, salt, pepper, and parsley until well blended. Add the macaroni and cheese. Mix lightly. Shape into a loaf. Place in an oiled pan and brush with the oil. Bake in a 375° oven 35 minutes.
Serves 4–6.

SPAGHETTI WITH VEAL AND PEPPERS

3 *tablespoons butter*
1½ *pounds boneless veal,
    cut into ½-inch cubes*
1½ *teaspoons salt*
¼ *teaspoon dried ground
    red peppers*
½ *teaspoon orégano*
2 *tablespoons flour*
1 *cup beef broth*

1½ *pounds tomatoes,
    chopped*
½ *cup Marsala wine or
    sweet sherry*
4 *tablespoons olive oil*
1½ *cups thinly sliced onions*
1 *clove garlic, minced*
4 *green peppers, sliced*
1 *pound spaghetti,
    cooked and drained*

Melt the butter in a saucepan; sauté the veal, salt, red peppers, and orégano until browned, stirring frequently. Sprinkle with the flour. Add the broth, stirring constantly until the boiling point. Mix in the tomatoes and wine. Cook over low heat 30 minutes, stirring occasionally.

Heat the oil in a skillet; sauté the onions, garlic, and green peppers 10 minutes, stirring occasionally. Mix into the veal mixture. Cook 10 minutes longer.

Heap the spaghetti on a hot platter. Pour the veal mixture on top and serve.

Serves 4–6.

SCALOPPINE WITH VEGETABLES

3 *tomatoes, peeled and*
    diced
4 *tablespoons olive oil*
1½ *cups chopped onions*
2 *green peppers, cut*
    julienne
1 *cup beef broth*
½ *pound green peas,*
    shelled

2 *carrots*
1½ *teaspoons salt*
¼ *teaspoon freshly ground*
    black pepper
½ *teaspoon basil*
12 *veal scallops*
1 *pound spaghetti,*
    cooked and drained

Cook the tomatoes over low heat 10 minutes.

Heat 2 tablespoons of the olive oil in a skillet; sauté the onions and green peppers 10 minutes. Add the tomatoes, broth, peas, carrots, salt, pepper, and basil. Cook over low heat 10 minutes, stirring occasionally.

Heat the remaining olive oil in a skillet; sauté the veal until browned on both sides. Combine with the vegetables. Cook 10 minutes, or until tender. Taste for seasoning.

Heap the spaghetti on a platter. Arrange the veal over it and pour the sauce on top.

Serves 4–6.

VEAL SCALOPPINE AND NOODLE CASSEROLE

1 *pound thin veal cutlet,*
  cut into 12 *pieces*
1½ *teaspoons salt*
¾ *teaspoon freshly ground*
  black pepper
3 *tablespoons butter*
1 *clove garlic*
½ *pound mushrooms,*
  sliced

1 *cup dry white wine*
½ *pound medium noodles,*
  cooked and drained
1 *cup sour cream*
¼ *pound Swiss cheese,*
  sliced
3 *tomatoes, sliced*
½ *cup grated Parmesan*
  cheese

Season the veal with ¾ teaspoon salt and ½ teaspoon pepper. Melt the butter in a skillet; add the veal and garlic. Sauté until veal is browned on both sides. Discard the garlic and add the mushrooms and ½ cup of the wine. Cover and cook over low heat 10 minutes.

Toss the noodles with the sour cream. In a 2-quart buttered casserole, arrange layers of half the noodles, veal mixture, Swiss cheese, and tomatoes. Sprinkle with half the remaining salt and pepper. Repeat the layers. Stir the remaining wine and the Parmesan cheese into the pan juices in the skillet. Bring to a boil, scraping the bottom, then pour into the casserole. Bake in a 400° oven 20 minutes.

Serves 4.

VEAL GOULASH CASSEROLE

4 tablespoons butter
1½ cups chopped onions
2 pounds boneless veal,
cut into ½-inch cubes
1 8-ounce can tomato
sauce
1½ teaspoons salt
2 teaspoons paprika

¼ teaspoon pepper
1 cup sour cream
4 tablespoons dry bread
crumbs
1 pound broad noodles,
cooked and drained
3 tablespoons melted
butter

Melt the butter in a skillet; sauté the onions and veal until browned. Mix in the tomato sauce, salt, paprika, and pepper. Cover and cook over low heat 45 minutes. Stir in the sour cream gradually. Taste for seasoning.

Dust a buttered casserole with some of the bread crumbs. Spread half the noodles on the bottom. Pour the veal mixture over the noodles and cover with the remaining noodles. Sprinkle with the remaining bread crumbs and the melted butter. Bake in a 375° oven for 15 minutes.

Serves 6–8.

HUNGARIAN MEAT BALLS WITH NOODLES

1 pound ground veal
1 teaspoon salt
¼ teaspoon white pepper
1 clove garlic, minced
2 tablespoons minced
parsley
1 egg, beaten
¼ cup milk
½ cup dry bread crumbs
¼ cup vegetable oil

¼ cup minced onion
1 cup sliced mushrooms
2 tablespoons flour
1 cup beef broth
1 cup sour cream
½ teaspoon paprika
1 8-ounce package broad
noodles, cooked and
drained
2 tablespoons poppy seeds

Mix together the veal, salt, pepper, garlic, parsley, egg, milk, and bread crumbs. Shape into ½-inch balls.

Heat the oil in a skillet; brown the meat balls; remove from pan. To the fat remaining, add the onion and mushrooms; sauté 5 minutes. Blend in the flour, then add the broth, stirring steadily to the boiling point. Return the meat balls. Cover and cook over low heat 20 minutes. Stir in the sour cream and paprika; heat, but do not let boil.

Toss the noodles with the poppy seeds in a heated serving dish. Pour the meat balls and gravy over them.

Serves 4–5.

SPAGHETTI WITH VEAL DUMPLINGS

(Spaghetti con Gnocchi di Vitello)

½ pound ground veal
⅛ pound prosciutto or cooked ham, finely chopped
2 tablespoons grated Parmesan cheese
1½ teaspoons salt
1 egg, beaten
½ cup dry bread crumbs

3 tablespoons butter
2 tablespoons dry vermouth
1 pound tomatoes, chopped
¼ teaspoon freshly ground black pepper
1 pound spaghetti, cooked and drained

Mix together the veal, ham, cheese, ½ teaspoon salt, and the egg. Shape teaspoonfuls of the mixture into little balls. Roll in the bread crumbs.

Melt the butter in a saucepan; brown the balls. Add the wine; cook until wine is absorbed. Add the tomatoes, pepper, and remaining salt; cook over low heat 30 minutes. Taste for seasoning. Pour over the hot spaghetti and serve with grated cheese.

Serves 4.

PORK STEW WITH NOODLES
(Tocana de Porc cu Tatei)

3 tablespoons olive oil
1½ pounds onions, peeled
    and sliced
1 pound sauerkraut,
    drained
2 pounds boneless pork,
    cubed
1 clove garlic, minced
2 teaspoons salt
½ teaspoon freshly ground
    black pepper

1 teaspoon thyme
2 tablespoons chopped
    parsley
1 tablespoon chopped dill
2 teaspoons caraway seeds
2 cups beef broth
1 tablespoon paprika
1 cup sour cream
1 pound medium noodles,
    cooked and drained

Heat 2 tablespoons of the oil in a skillet; sauté the onions 10 minutes, stirring frequently. Add the sauerkraut and cook over medium heat 5 minutes, stirring constantly.

Heat the remaining oil in a Dutch oven or heavy saucepan; brown the pork. Mix in the garlic, salt, pepper, thyme, parsley, dill, caraway seeds, and broth. Cover and cook over low heat 1½ hours, or until the pork is tender. Stir in the paprika and sour cream; cook 5 minutes. Add the noodles and mix together lightly. Taste for seasoning.

Serves 4–6.

PORK AND MACARONI SOUP-STEW

(Minestra Asciutta)

4 *cups boiling water*
1 *pound elbow macaroni*
2 *tablespoons olive oil*
1½ *pounds pork, cubed*
2 *cloves garlic, minced*

2 *tomatoes, chopped*
2 *cups beef broth*
1 *teaspoon salt*
¼ *teaspoon freshly ground black pepper*

Pour the boiling water over the macaroni; let soak 10 minutes, stirring frequently. Drain well.

Heat the olive oil in a large saucepan. Add the pork and garlic and brown lightly, stirring frequently. Mix in the tomatoes, broth, salt, pepper, and macaroni. Cook over low heat 30 minutes, stirring occasionally. Taste for seasoning. The resulting dish has more liquid than the usual stew.

Serves 6–8.

PORK-MACARONI CASSEROLE

1½ *pounds boneless pork, cut into ½-inch cubes*
¼ *cup sifted flour*
2 *teaspoons salt*
¼ *teaspoon pepper*
¼ *teaspoon thyme*
2 *tablespoons vegetable oil*

½ *pound macaroni, cooked and drained*
3 *tablespoons melted butter*
¼ *cup grated Parmesan cheese*

Dip the pork cubes into a mixture of the flour, salt, pepper, and thyme, coating the pieces well.

Heat the oil in a skillet; brown the pork on all sides. Drain well. Mix together the pork, macaroni, melted butter, and grated cheese. Turn into a buttered casserole. Bake in a 375° oven 20 minutes.

Serves 4–6.

PORK AND NOODLE CASSEROLE

3 tablespoons peanut or
  vegetable oil
2 pounds pork, diced
1½ cups thinly sliced onions
1 green pepper, cut
  julienne
1 cup chicken broth
2 cloves garlic, minced
2 teaspoons soy sauce

½ teaspoon freshly ground
  black pepper
¼ pound mushrooms,
  sliced
2 pimientos, sliced
¼ cup chopped parsley
1 pound broad noodles,
  cooked and drained
2 tablespoons butter

Heat the oil in a large saucepan; lightly brown the pork. Mix in the onions, green pepper, and broth. Cook over low heat 30 minutes. Stir in the garlic, soy sauce, pepper, and mushrooms. Cook 10 minutes, stirring occasionally. Mix in the pimientos and parsley. Taste for seasoning.

In a buttered casserole, arrange several successive layers of the noodles and pork mixture. Dot with the butter. Bake in a 425° oven 15 minutes.

Serves 4–6.

SPAGHETTI-PORK CASSEROLE

1 tablespoon vegetable
  oil
1 pound boneless pork,
  cut into ½-inch cubes
1½ teaspoons salt
½ teaspoon freshly ground
  black pepper
1 cup chopped onions

½ cup diced celery
1 19-ounce can tomatoes
3 tablespoons soy sauce
½ pound spaghetti, cooked
  and drained
1 cup (¼ pound) grated
  cheddar cheese

Heat the oil in a skillet; brown the pork. Add the salt, pepper, onions, and celery; cook 5 minutes, stirring frequently. Mix in the tomatoes and soy sauce. Bring to a boil, cover, and cook over low heat 30 minutes. Add the spaghetti; mix lightly and taste for seasoning. Turn into a greased 2-quart casserole. Sprinkle with the cheese. Bake in a preheated 350° oven 25 minutes.

Serves 4.

INDONESIAN FRIED NOODLES

(Bahmi Goreng)

½ *pound mie (Chinese vermicelli), vermicelli, or fine egg noodles*
2 *eggs, beaten*
¾ *cup oil*
1 *pound pork, cut julienne*
1½ *cups thinly sliced onions*
2 *cloves garlic, minced*
2 *teaspoons minced ginger root or 1 table-spoon powdered ginger*
3 *cups shredded Chinese or green cabbage*
1 *cup bean sprouts*
1 *cup diced cooked or canned shrimp*
¼ *cup chopped green onions*
1 *tablespoon soy sauce*
½ *teaspoon freshly ground black pepper*

Cook the noodles in boiling salted water until almost tender. Drain and spread on a flat surface to cool and dry. If possible, chill 2 hours. Make an omelet of the eggs. Roll up and slice fine.

Heat 2 tablespoons oil in a skillet; sauté the pork 10 minutes. Remove and keep warm. Heat 2 tablespoons oil in the same skillet; sauté the onions, garlic, and ginger 3 minutes. Remove and keep warm. Heat 2 tablespoons oil in the same skillet; sauté the cabbage and bean sprouts 3 minutes. Add the shrimp and sauté 2 minutes. Return all the sautéed ingredients and add the green onions, soy sauce, and pepper. Cook 2 minutes.

In a separate skillet, heat the remaining oil; turn the noodles into it and fry until browned. Drain. Heap the noodles on a platter and turn out the pork mixture over them. Sprinkle with the sliced omelet.

Serves 4–6.

FRIED NOODLES AND PORK

½ *pound boneless pork*
4 *eggs*
2 *teaspoons salt*
¾ *cup vegetable oil*
½ *pound mushrooms, sliced*
½ *cup sliced green onions*
½ *cup sliced water chestnuts*
2 *tablespoons soy sauce*

2 *tablespoons dry sherry*
1 *teaspoon monosodium glutamate*
Chinese Noodles (see recipe) or ½ pound fine noodles, cooked and drained

Cut the pork into matchlike pieces. Beat the eggs and ½ teaspoon salt. Heat 2 tablespoons oil in a 9-inch skillet. Pour in the eggs; cook until set and browned on both sides. Turn out onto a plate and cut into narrow strips.

Heat 3 tablespoons oil in the skillet and brown the pork. Add the mushrooms, green onions, and water chestnuts. Cook over medium heat 5 minutes, stirring frequently. Mix in the soy sauce, sherry, and monosodium glutamate. Keep hot while preparing the noodles.

Heat the remaining oil in a skillet. Add the cooked noodles and remaining salt. Cook over high heat, stirring almost constantly, until browned, about 5 minutes. Heap in a bowl, cover with the pork mixture, and sprinkle with the egg strips.

Serves 2–4.

CHINESE FRIED NOODLES WITH PORK

1 8-ounce package fine
   noodles
⅓ cup vegetable oil
1 pound pork, cut into
   small dice
½ pound mushrooms,
   sliced

2 tablespoons cornstarch
3 tablespoons soy sauce
1½ cups beef broth
1 cup bean sprouts
½ teaspoon salt
3 tablespoons chopped
   green onions

Cook the noodles in boiling salted water 2 minutes less than package directs. Drain well and spread on a large plate. Chill 2–3 hours.

Heat half the oil in a skillet; add the pork. Cook over high heat, stirring almost constantly until browned. Mix in the mushrooms; cook 3 minutes. Mix the cornstarch with the soy sauce and add with the broth, stirring steadily to the boiling point. Cook 5 minutes. Add the bean sprouts and salt; cook 5 minutes longer.

In a separate large skillet, heat the remaining oil until it smokes. Turn the noodles into it and form into a pancake. Fry until browned, then turn over in one piece and brown the other side. Turn out onto a hot platter. Pour the pork mixture on top and sprinkle with the onions.

Serves 4–5.

CHINESE PORK AND SOFT NOODLES
(Lo Mein)

1 *pound boneless pork*	4 *tablespoons soy sauce*
4 *tablespoons oil*	1 *teaspoon sugar*
2 *teaspoons salt*	2 *tablespoons cornstarch*
¼ *teaspoon pepper*	1½ *cups chicken broth*
2 *cups sliced Chinese or*	3 *cups cooked and*
green cabbage	*drained fine noodles*
2 *cups sliced celery*	3 *green onions, chopped*
2 *cups bean sprouts*	

Cut the pork into matchlike pieces. Heat the oil in a deep skillet; sauté the meat 5 minutes. Add the salt, pepper, cabbage, celery, bean sprouts, soy sauce, and sugar. Mix well; cover and cook over low heat 3 minutes. Mix together the cornstarch and broth; stir into the mixture until thickened. Add the noodles; mix lightly and heat. Sprinkle with the green onions.

Serves 4 6.

PORK CHOW MEIN

3 *quarts water*	1½ *cups sliced onions*
2 *teaspoons salt*	1 *cup sliced celery*
1 *pound fine noodles (Chinese style, if available)*	¼ *pound mushrooms, sliced*
Vegetable oil for deep-fat frying	2 *cups bean sprouts*
	1 *tablespoon cornstarch*
4 *tablespoons peanut or vegetable oil*	2 *cups beef broth*
	½ *teaspoon sugar*
1 *pound pork, cut into small dice*	1 *tablespoon soy sauce*

Bring the water and salt to a boil. Add the noodles. Boil 2 minutes. Drain and rinse with cold water. Drain and dry as thoroughly as possible. Heat the deep oil to 375°. Place the noodles in a wire basket and fry until crisp and brown, about 3 minutes. Drain.

Heat the peanut oil in a saucepan. Sauté the pork 10 minutes, stirring frequently. Add the onions, celery, mushrooms, and bean sprouts. Sauté 5 minutes, stirring occasionally.

Mix the cornstarch with 2 tablespoons of the broth to a smooth paste. Add the remaining broth, the sugar and soy sauce. Pour over the pork mixture, stirring constantly to the boiling point.

Heap the noodles on a hot serving dish and pour the pork mixture over them.

Serves 4–6.

LASAGNE, NEOPOLITAN STYLE

(Lasagne al Forno, Napoletana)

1 tablespoon olive oil	1¼ teaspoons salt
1 pound pork, cut into	½ teaspoon black pepper
½-inch dice	1 pound lasagne or broad
½ cup chopped onions	noodles, cooked and
1 clove garlic, minced	drained
1 teaspoon minced	1 pound ricotta cheese
parsley	½ cup grated Parmesan
1½ cans tomato paste	cheese
2 cups warm water	

Heat the oil in a skillet; brown the pork, onions, garlic, and parsley. Mix the tomato paste with the water and add. Season with the salt and pepper. Cover and cook over low heat 1½ hours, adding a little water from time to time if necessary. This should make about 2 cups of tomato sauce. Taste for seasoning.

In a shallow greased casserole, arrange as many layers as possible of the *lasagne,* sauce, ricotta, and Parmesan; end with layers of sauce, ricotta, and Parmesan. Bake in a 350° oven 25 minutes.

Serves 6–8.

SMOKED PORK AND SPAGHETTI

1 tablespoon bacon fat
½ pound smoked pork butt
   or ham, cubed
¾ cup chopped onions
1½ pounds tomatoes, peeled
   and cubed

½ teaspoon freshly ground
   black pepper
1 pound spaghetti,
   cooked and drained
1 cup grated Parmesan
   cheese

Heat the bacon fat in a skillet. Sauté the pork and onions 15 minutes, stirring frequently. Mix in the tomatoes and pepper. Cover and cook over low heat 30 minutes. Taste for seasoning.

Pour the sauce over the spaghetti. Sprinkle the cheese on top and serve.

Serves 4–6.

SPAGHETTI WITH NEAPOLITAN MEAT SAUCE

2 tablespoons olive oil
1 pound boneless pork, cut
   into small cubes
¾ cup chopped onions
2 tablespoons minced
   parsley
2 cloves garlic, minced

2 6-ounce cans tomato
   paste
3 cups water
1 teaspoon salt
½ teaspoon freshly ground
   black pepper
1 pound spaghetti, cooked
   and drained

Heat the olive oil in a saucepan. Sauté the pork, onions, and parsley 15 minutes, mixing occasionally. Add the garlic, tomato paste, water, salt, and pepper. Cover and cook over low heat 2½ hours. Stir frequently, adding a little water if sauce becomes too thick. Taste for seasoning. Pour over the spaghetti and serve.

Serves 4–6.

PORK AND BEEF BALLS WITH SPAGHETTI

4 slices white bread,
  trimmed
¾ cup water
½ pound ground pork
½ pound ground beef
1 egg, beaten
2 tablespoons grated
  Parmesan cheese
2 tablespoons chopped
  parsley
2 tablespoons grated onion
1 clove garlic, minced

1 teaspoon salt
½ teaspoon freshly ground
  black pepper
¼ cup olive oil
¾ cup sliced onions
1 29-ounce can tomatoes
3 tablespoons tomato paste
1 bay leaf
1 teaspoon basil
3 tablespoons butter
1 pound spaghetti, cooked
  and drained

Soak the bread in the water 5 minutes. Press dry and mash the bread. Combine with the pork, beef, egg, cheese, parsley, grated onion, garlic, ½ teaspoon of the salt, and ¼ teaspoon of the pepper. Mix well and shape into 1-inch balls. Heat the oil in a skillet and brown the meat balls.

Combine the sliced onions, tomatoes, tomato paste, bay leaf, and remaining salt and pepper in a saucepan. Bring to a boil and add the meat balls. Cook over low heat 1 hour. Add the basil and butter and cook 5 minutes. Heap the spaghetti on a platter and pour the sauce over it.

Serves 4.

RUMANIAN PORK AND NOODLE PUDDING

(Musaca cu Tatei)

1 slice white bread, trimmed	1 pound fine noodles, cooked and drained
¼ cup milk	4 eggs, beaten
1 pound twice-ground pork	4 tablespoons butter
½ cup chopped parsley	½ cup heavy cream
1 cup grated onions	⅓ cup grated Parmesan cheese
3 teaspoons salt	
½ teaspoon freshly ground black pepper	

Soak the bread in the milk 5 minutes; mash smooth. Mix together the bread, pork, 2 tablespoons of the parsley, 2 tablespoons of the grated onions, 1½ teaspoons of the salt, and ¼ teaspoon of the pepper.

Mix the noodles with 2 of the eggs and the remaining salt and pepper. In a buttered casserole, arrange successive layers of the noodles and pork mixture; sprinkle the noodle layers with the remaining parsley and onions and dot with the butter. Make as many layers as possible, starting and ending with the noodles. Bake in a 350° oven 35 minutes.

Beat the remaining 2 eggs with the cream and cheese. Pour over the noodles and bake 20 minutes longer, or until the mixture is set and lightly browned on top.

Serves 4–6.

PORK CHOPS WITH SPAGHETTI

2 teaspoons salt	3 tablespoons butter
1 teaspoon freshly ground black pepper	1 pound spaghetti, cooked and drained
1 clove garlic, minced	2 cups grated cheddar
6 pork chops	cheese

Mix the salt, pepper, and garlic to a smooth paste. Rub the pork chops with the mixture. Melt the butter in a skillet and brown the chops on both sides. Drain.

Spread the spaghetti in a greased baking dish. Sprinkle 1 cup of the cheese over it. Arrange the chops on top. Bake in a 350° oven 20 minutes. Sprinkle the remaining cheese over the chops. Bake 15 minutes longer.

Serves 6.

MACARONI AND HAM CASSEROLE

3 tablespoons butter	1 cup chopped boiled ham
3 tablespoons flour	2 cups grated cheddar
2 cups milk	cheese
1 teaspoon salt	½ cup bread crumbs
¼ teaspoon pepper	¼ cup melted butter
½ pound macaroni, cooked and drained	

Melt the 3 tablespoons butter in a saucepan. Blend in the flour until smooth. Gradually add the milk, stirring constantly to the boiling point. Add salt and pepper. Cook over low heat 5 minutes.

In a buttered casserole, arrange alternate layers of the macaroni, ham, cheese, and sauce, ending with the sauce. Mix the bread crumbs and melted butter, and sprinkle over top layer. Bake in a 350° oven 25 minutes.

Serves 3–4.

EGG NOODLES WITH HAM

(Tagliatelle alla Bolognese con Prosciutto)

4 tablespoons butter
¼ pound prosciutto ham,
   cut julienne
1 cup grated Parmesan
   cheese

½ Egg-Noodle Dough
   recipe or ½ pound
   medium egg noodles,
   cooked and drained

Melt the butter in a skillet; sauté the ham 3 minutes. Toss the hot noodles with the cheese, then with the ham-butter sauce.
Serves 2–3.

ITALIAN HAM CUSTARD

1 29-ounce can tomatoes
2 onions, chopped
1½ teaspoons salt
¼ teaspoon pepper
2 tablespoons bread
   crumbs
1 pound macaroni,
   cooked and drained

¾ pound Parma or
   prosciutto ham,
   coarsely shredded
½ pound mushrooms,
   sliced
1½ cups grated Parmesan
   cheese
¼ pound butter
3 eggs
1½ cups light cream

Combine the tomatoes, onions, salt, and pepper and cook 10 minutes. Purée in an electric blender or force through a sieve. Butter a casserole and dust with the bread crumbs. Arrange successive layers (using half of each ingredient) of the macaroni, ham, mushrooms, tomato mixture, cheese, and dots of butter. Repeat the layers with remaining ingredients. Beat together the eggs and cream. Pour over the top. Bake in a 350° oven 35 minutes.
Serves 4–6.

MACARONI MILANAISE

2 tablespoons olive oil
½ pound ham, chopped
1 cup finely chopped
  onions
2 cloves garlic, minced
1 6-ounce can tomato paste
2 cups beef broth
1 cup water
½ teaspoon basil

2 tablespoons chopped
  parsley
1 bay leaf
½ teaspoon salt
¼ teaspoon dried ground
  red peppers
2 cups grated Parmesan
  cheese
1 pound elbow macaroni,
  cooked and drained

Heat the olive oil in a skillet. Add the ham, onions, and garlic; sauté 10 minutes, stirring frequently. Add the tomato paste, broth, water, basil, parsley, bay leaf, salt, and dried peppers; bring to a boil and cook over low heat 2 hours.

Discard the bay leaf. Add the cheese and cook 5 minutes, stirring frequently. Taste for seasoning.

Put the macaroni in a hot bowl and pour the sauce over it. *Serves 4–6.*

PAPRIKA MACARONI

2 cups sour cream, scalded
½ pound cooked ham,
  ground
½ teaspoon freshly ground
  black pepper
2 teaspoons paprika
2 teaspoons chopped
  parsley

1 pound elbow macaroni,
  cooked and drained
½ pound cottage cheese,
  drained
1 teaspoon salt
3 tablespoons melted
  butter

Mix the sour cream, ham, pepper, paprika, parsley, and macaroni until well blended. Pour into a buttered baking dish.

Force the cottage cheese through a sieve; add salt and spread over macaroni mixture. Pour the melted butter over the top. Bake in a 325° oven 20 minutes.

Serves 4–6.

HAM CASSEROLE, SOUTHERN STYLE

3 tablespoons butter
3 tablespoons flour
1½ cups milk
1 teaspoon salt
¼ teaspoon freshly ground
  black pepper
3 stalks celery, chopped

½ pound cooked ham,
  ground
½ pound elbow macaroni,
  cooked and drained
3 apples, peeled and
  sliced thin
⅓ cup brown sugar

Melt the butter in a saucepan; blend in the flour until smooth. Gradually add the milk, stirring constantly to the boiling point. Add the salt, pepper, and celery; cook over low heat 5 minutes. Mix in the ham and macaroni. Taste for seasoning. Pour into a buttered casserole and arrange the apple slices on top. Sprinkle with the brown sugar. Place the casserole in a pan of water. Bake in a 350° oven 30 minutes.

Serves 4.

SPAGHETTI WITH DEVILED HAM

4 tablespoons butter
½ cup grated onions
3 tablespoons flour
3 cups milk, scalded
2 cans deviled ham
2 teaspoons Worcester-
  shire sauce

⅛ teaspoon freshly ground
  black pepper
½ teaspoon dry mustard
1 pound spaghetti, cooked
  and drained
½ cup grated Gruyère
  cheese
¼ cup bread crumbs

Melt the butter in a saucepan. Sauté the onions 5 minutes, stirring frequently. Blend in the flour. Add the milk, stirring constantly to the boiling point, then cook over low heat 5 minutes. Mix in the deviled ham, Worcestershire sauce, pepper, and mustard. Add the spaghetti, tossing until well blended.

Pour the mixture into a buttered baking dish. Sprinkle the cheese and bread crumbs on top. Bake in a 350° oven 20 minutes. *Serves 4–6.*

BACON AND NOODLE CASSEROLE

¾ pound bacon
1 pound broad noodles,
　cooked and drained
1½ cups cottage cheese,
　drained
3 tablespoons grated
　onion

2 pimientos, cut julienne
1 teaspoon salt
½ teaspoon freshly ground
　black pepper
¼ cup dry bread crumbs
3 tablespoons butter

Fry the bacon until crisp. Drain well and crumble.

Mix together the noodles, cottage cheese, onion, pimientos, salt, and pepper. Fold in the bacon. Pour into a buttered casserole. Sprinkle the bread crumbs on top and dot with the butter. Bake in a 350° oven 20 minutes.

Serves 4–6.

SPAGHETTI WITH BACON SAUCE

½ pound bacon, diced
2 cloves garlic, minced
1 teaspoon crushed black
　peppercorns

1 pound spaghetti, cooked
　and drained
½ cup grated Parmesan
　cheese

Combine the bacon and garlic in a skillet. Fry until the bacon is crisp. Mix in the crushed peppercorns and remove from the heat. Pour over the spaghetti, sprinkle with the cheese, and serve at once.

Serves 4–6.

MACARONI-STUFFED SPARERIBS

2 *racks of spareribs*
2½ *teaspoons salt*
1 *teaspoon freshly ground*
　black pepper
2 *tablespoons flour*
1 *16-ounce can pineapple*
　chunks, drained

1 *green pepper, cut*
　julienne
1 *teaspoon soy sauce*
2 *tablespoons brown sugar*
¼ *teaspoon powdered ginger*
½ *pound elbow macaroni,*
　cooked and drained

Rub the spareribs with a mixture of the salt, pepper, and flour. Mix together the pineapple, green pepper, soy sauce, brown sugar, ginger, and macaroni. Spread over 1 rack of spareribs and cover with the other. Fasten the edges with skewers or toothpicks. Place on a rack in a shallow roasting pan. Roast in a 350° oven 2¼ hours, or until the ribs are tender.
Serves 4–6.

LAMB AND MACARONI

¼ *cup butter*
1 *cup chopped onions*
1 *clove garlic, minced*
2 *pounds boneless lamb,*
　cut into 1-inch cubes
1 *6-ounce can tomato paste*
1 *cup water*

2 *tomatoes, chopped*
2 *teaspoons salt*
½ *teaspoon freshly ground*
　black pepper
½ *teaspoon thyme*
1 *pound macaroni, half*
　cooked and drained

Melt the butter in a saucepan; sauté the onions, garlic, and lamb until browned. Add the tomato paste, water, tomatoes, salt, pepper, and thyme. Cover and cook over low heat 1 hour, or until the lamb is tender.
Stir in the macaroni. Cook 10 minutes. Taste for seasoning.
Serves 6–8.

BAKED ARABIC MACARONI

4 tablespoons butter
1½ cups finely chopped
   onions
2 pounds lamb or beef,
   ground twice
3 teaspoons salt
1 teaspoon pepper

1 teaspoon cinnamon
1 pound macaroni, half
   cooked
2 cups tomato juice
½ cup grated Parmesan
   cheese

Melt the butter in a large skillet; sauté the onions 5 minutes, stirring frequently. Add the meat, 2 teaspoons of the salt, the pepper and cinnamon. Sauté 15 minutes, stirring frequently.

Place the half-cooked macaroni in a buttered baking dish. Add the meat mixture and stir together gently. Add the tomato juice and remaining salt. Bake in a 350° oven 30 minutes. Add a little water if the mixture becomes too dry.

Sprinkle with the grated cheese before serving.

Serves 6–8.

LAMB CURRY CASSEROLE

4 tablespoons butter
1 cup chopped onions
1½ pounds lamb, cut into
   1-inch cubes
1½ teaspoons salt
¼ teaspoon freshly ground
   black pepper
1 tablespoon curry
   powder

2 tablespoons flour
2 cups beef broth
1 teaspoon drained capers
1 cup milk
1 pound spaghetti, cooked
   and drained
2 tablespoons olive oil

Melt the butter in a saucepan; sauté the onions, lamb, salt, pepper, and curry powder 15 minutes, stirring frequently. Blend in the flour. Gradually add the broth, stirring constantly to the boiling point. Cook over low heat 45 minutes, or until the lamb is tender. Add the capers and milk. Cook 5 minutes, stirring occasionally. Taste for seasoning.

Spread half the spaghetti in a buttered baking dish. Pour the lamb mixture over it and cover with the remaining spaghetti. Sprinkle the olive oil on top. Bake in a 375° oven 20 minutes.

Serves 4–6.

RAVIOLI WITH LAMB AND SPINACH

(Agnolotti)

3 *cups sifted flour*	1 *cup grated Parmesan*
¼ *teaspoon salt*	*cheese*
1 *tablespoon melted butter*	⅛ *pound salami, chopped*
2 *eggs, beaten*	(*Italian, if available*)
½ *cup warm water*	¼ *teaspoon freshly ground*
1 *cup cooked chopped*	*black pepper*
lamb	¼ *teaspoon nutmeg*
1 *cup cooked chopped*	1 *egg yolk, beaten*
spinach	½ *cup melted butter*

Sift the flour and salt onto a board. Make a well in the center. Pour 1 tablespoon melted butter, eggs, and water into it. Work in the flour, kneading until a medium-soft and smooth dough is formed. Cover and let stand 15 minutes. Roll out as thin as possible. Cut into 4-inch squares.

Mix together the lamb, spinach, 2 tablespoons Parmesan cheese, salami, pepper, nutmeg, and egg yolk. Place a tablespoonful of the lamb mixture on each square. Fold over the dough, sealing the edges well.

Drop into boiling salted water. Boil 10 minutes. Drain well. Serve with the melted butter and remaining cheese.

Serves 6–8.

SPAGHETTI WITH THREE MEATS
(Spaghetti Turbigo)

4 *tablespoons olive oil*	½ *pound cooked tongue,*
2 *cloves garlic, minced*	*cut julienne*
1½ *pounds tomatoes, peeled*	¼ *pound cooked ham, cut*
and chopped	*julienne*
1 *teaspoon salt*	1½ *cups thinly sliced onions*
¼ *teaspoon freshly ground*	¾ *cup grated Parmesan*
black pepper	*cheese*
1 *pound spaghetti,*	3 *spicy sausages (Spanish*
cooked and drained	*style, if available),*
4 *tablespoons melted*	*sliced, half cooked,*
butter	*and drained*

Heat the olive oil in a saucepan; sauté the garlic 2 minutes. Add the tomatoes, salt, and pepper. Cover and cook over low heat 20 minutes, stirring occasionally. Mash very smooth. Taste for seasoning.

Mix the spaghetti and melted butter together. In a buttered casserole, arrange as many successive layers as possible of the spaghetti, tongue, ham, onions, tomato sauce, and cheese, ending with the cheese. Arrange the slices of sausage on top. Bake in a 350° oven 30 minutes.

Serves 4–6.

SPAGHETTI WITH SWEETBREADS

3 *pairs calves' sweetbreads*
2 *cups water*
2 *tablespoons vinegar*
2 *teaspoons salt*
1 *bay leaf*
1 *onion*

¼ *pound (1 stick) butter*
2 *tablespoons flour*
½ *cup heavy cream*
2 *cups sliced mushrooms*
1 *pound thin spaghetti,*
    cooked and drained

Wash the sweetbreads thoroughly and let soak in cold water ½ hour. Drain. Combine the sweetbreads, the 2 cups water, the vinegar, salt, bay leaf, and onion in a saucepan. Cook over medium heat 15 minutes. Drain, reserving 1 cup of the stock. Remove the membrane from the sweetbreads and cut into small cubes.

Melt half the butter in a saucepan. Blend in the flour. Gradually add the reserved stock and the cream, stirring constantly to the boiling point. Cook over low heat 5 minutes, stirring occasionally.

Melt the remaining butter in a skillet. Add the mushrooms and sauté 10 minutes, stirring frequently. Combine the sweetbreads, sauce, and mushrooms and mix together. Taste for seasoning. Cook over low heat until very hot.

Heap the spaghetti on a platter and pour the sauce over it. Serve immediately.

Serves 4–6.

SPAGHETTI WITH SWEETBREADS AND TONGUE

(Spaghetti Lucernoise)

1½ cups sifted flour
1½ teaspoons salt
½ pound (2 sticks) butter
4 tablespoons sour cream
½ pound spaghetti, broken
    into 2-inch lengths,
    cooked and drained

2 pairs sweetbreads,
    cooked, drained, and
    diced
½ pound cooked tongue,
    diced
2 egg yolks
1 cup heavy cream
3 tablespoons dry sherry

Sift the flour and ½ teaspoon salt into a bowl. Cut in the butter (reserving 4 tablespoons) until the consistency of coarse sand. Add the sour cream, tossing lightly until a ball of dough is formed. Let chill at least 2 hours, or overnight if possible. Roll out the dough thin and line a 2-quart casserole with it. The scraps may be saved for strips across the top.

Melt the reserved butter. Add the spaghetti and toss lightly. Arrange as many layers as possible of the spaghetti, sweetbreads, and tongue in the lined casserole.

Beat together the egg yolks, cream, sherry, and remaining salt; pour over the contents of the casserole. Roll out the remaining dough and arrange in a lattice design on top.

Bake in a 425° oven 15 minutes. Reduce heat to 375° and bake 20 minutes longer, or until the custard is set and the crust is lightly browned. Cut into pie-shaped wedges and serve hot.

Serves 4–6.

TIMBALE OF GREEN NOODLES
AND SWEETBREADS

(Timballo Verde)

2 *dried mushrooms*
4 *tablespoons butter*
¼ *pound sweetbreads,*
  cooked and cubed
⅛ *pound ham, cubed*
¼ *pound chicken livers,*
  diced
¼ *pound mushrooms, sliced*
1 *cup Bolognese Sauce*
  (*see recipe*), *strained*

½ *cup tomato sauce*
2 *truffles, sliced*
1 *cup Béchamel Sauce*
  (*see recipe*)
1 *pound green noodles,*
  cooked and drained
1 *cup grated Parmesan*
  cheese
4 *tablespoons dry bread*
  crumbs

Soak the dried mushrooms in water 10 minutes. Drain and slice.

Melt the butter in a skillet; stir in the sweetbreads, ham, livers, and mushrooms. Sauté 5 minutes. Add the Bolognese and tomato sauces; cook over low heat 10 minutes. Taste for seasoning. Mix in the truffles. Remove about a third of this sauce and reserve.

Combine the balance of the sauce with the Béchamel Sauce, noodles, and half the Parmesan cheese. Mix thoroughly.

Butter 4–6 individual baking dishes and sprinkle with the bread crumbs. Divide the noodle mixture among them. Cover with the reserved sauce and sprinkle with remaining cheese. Bake in a 375° oven 10 minutes.

Serves 4–6.

BAKED LASAGNE

(Lasagne al Forno)

4 tablespoons butter
2 tablespoons flour
1½ teaspoons salt
¾ cup milk
½ pound chicken livers,
    diced
½ pound Italian sausages,
    skinned and chopped
2 tablespoons olive oil

Lasagne dough (see recipe),
    or 1 pound lasagne,
    cooked and drained
3 cups Tomato Sauce
    (see recipe)
½ pound prosciutto or
    cooked ham, chopped
1½ cups grated Parmesan
    cheese

Melt 2 tablespoons butter in a saucepan; blend in the flour and half the salt. Add the milk, stirring steadily to the boiling point, then cook over low heat 5 minutes.

Melt 1 tablespoon butter in a skillet; sauté the livers 2 minutes. Add the sausage meat and cook 10 minutes. Drain.

Oil a shallow baking dish and make a layer of *lasagne*. Arrange as many layers as possible of the Tomato Sauce, ham, sausage mixture, white sauce, grated cheese, and *lasagne*. End with *lasagne* and grated cheese. Dot with the remaining butter. Bake in a 400° oven 15 minutes, or until browned. Cut into squares and serve from the dish.

Serves 4–6.

MACARONI AND LIVER AU GRATIN

6 tablespoons butter
1½ cups chopped onions
1 29-ounce can tomatoes
2 tablespoons tomato paste
2 teaspoons salt
⅛ teaspoon dried ground red peppers

1 pound chicken livers, diced
½ pound mushrooms, sliced
1 pound macaroni, cooked and drained
¼ cup dry bread crumbs
½ cup grated Gruyère or Swiss cheese

Melt half the butter in a saucepan; sauté the onions 5 minutes, stirring frequently. Mix in the tomatoes, tomato paste, salt, and dried peppers. Cook over low heat 45 minutes, stirring occasionally.

Melt the remaining butter in a skillet; sauté the chicken livers and mushrooms 5 minutes, stirring frequently. Add to the sauce. Cook 5 minutes. Taste for seasoning.

Spread the macaroni in a buttered casserole. Cover with the sauce. Sprinkle a mixture of the bread crumbs and cheese on top. Bake in a 350° oven 25 minutes.

Serves 4–6.

SAUSAGE CASSEROLE

8 spicy sausages (Italian or Spanish, if available), cut into 1-inch slices
1½ cups chopped onions
2 green peppers, cut julienne

1 10½-ounce can condensed tomato soup
½ cup water
1 pound spaghetti, cooked and drained

Fry the sausages in a skillet 5 minutes. Remove the sausages and pour off all but 2 tablespoons of the fat. Add the onions and green peppers to the fat and sauté 10 minutes, stirring frequently. Mix the soup and water. Add to the vegetables. Bring to a boil and cook over low heat 5 minutes. Mix in the spaghetti and sausages. Pour the mixture into a buttered baking dish. Bake in a 350° oven 30 minutes.

Serves 4–6.

YUCATAN MACARONI

¾ *pound pork sausage meat*
¾ *cup diced onions*
¾ *cup diced green peppers*
2 *19-ounce cans tomatoes*
1 *teaspoon salt*
1 *tablespoon chili powder*
2 *teaspoons sugar*
½ *pound elbow macaroni*
2 *cups sour cream*

In a large skillet, sauté the sausage meat, onions, and green peppers until brown. Pour off the fat. Mix in the tomatoes, salt, chili powder, and sugar. Bring to a boil. Add the macaroni; cover and cook over low heat 25 minutes. Blend in the sour cream. Heat, but do not let boil. Taste for seasoning.

Serves 2–3.

MACARONI-SAUSAGE CASSEROLE

⅓ *cup vegetable oil*
¾ *cup thinly sliced onions*
1 *clove garlic, minced*
¾ *cup chopped green peppers*
1½ *teaspoons salt*
1 *bay leaf, finely crushed*
¾ *pound elbow macaroni*
1 *10½-ounce can condensed cream of mushroom soup*
1 *cup boiling water*
1 *19-ounce can tomatoes*
¼ *teaspoon freshly ground black pepper*
8 *pork sausages*
½ *cup grated Parmesan cheese*

Heat the oil in a casserole; sauté the onions, garlic, green peppers, salt, and bay leaf until lightly browned. Add the uncooked macaroni; cook, stirring almost constantly, until macaroni browns lightly. Stir in the mushroom soup, water, tomatoes, and pepper. Bring to a boil; cover and cook over low heat 20 minutes, stirring a few times. While the macaroni is cooking, brown the sausages in a skillet. Drain.

Sprinkle the macaroni with the cheese and arrange sausages on top.

Serves 4.

VERMICELLI WITH SAUSAGE SAUCE

1 *pound sweet Italian sausage, sliced into ¼-inch pieces*	1 *teaspoon basil*
	½ *teaspoon salt*
	¼ *teaspoon freshly ground black pepper*
1½ *cups chopped onions*	
1 *clove garlic, minced*	½ *cup chopped black olives*
1 *pound mushrooms, sliced*	1 *pound vermicelli, cooked and drained*
1 *29-ounce can tomatoes*	

Cook the sausages in a skillet 5 minutes. Pour off all but 2 tablespoons of the fat. Add the onions and garlic; cook 10 minutes. Add the mushrooms; cook 5 minutes. Mix in the tomatoes, basil, salt, and pepper. Bring to a boil and cook over low heat 45 minutes, adding water if sauce becomes too thick. Stir in the olives. Taste for seasoning. Pour sauce over the vermicelli.

Serves 4–6.

PHILIPPINE STUFFED NOODLES IN STEW
(Pancit Molo)

NOODLES

1 *cup flour*	2 *egg yolks*
¼ *teaspoon salt*	1 *tablespoon water*

Sift the flour and salt into a bowl; work in the egg yolks and water with the fingers. Knead until smooth and elastic. Cover with a bowl and let stand while preparing the filling:

1 *pound ground pork*	½ *cup chopped green onions*
½ *pound raw shrimp,*	4 *cloves garlic, minced*
shelled, deveined,	½ *cup chopped water*
and chopped	*chestnuts*
1 *teaspoon anchovy paste*	3 *tablespoons oil*
1½ *teaspoons salt*	1 *cup chopped onions*
½ *teaspoon freshly ground*	6 *cups chicken broth*
black pepper	

Mix together the pork, shrimp, anchovy paste, salt, pepper, green onions, garlic, and water chestnuts. Roll out the dough paper-thin and cut into 3-inch squares. Place a heaping teaspoonful of the mixture on each and fold the dough into a triangle. Seal edges well. (You will have about two thirds of the pork mixture left.)

Heat the oil in a saucepan; sauté the onions 5 minutes. Add the remaining pork mixture and sauté 5 minutes. Stir in the broth and bring to a boil. Carefully drop the stuffed noodles into the broth. Cover and cook over low heat 15 minutes. Taste for seasoning and serve in deep bowls.

Serves 6–8.

CHILI CON CARNE CASSEROLE

3 tablespoons vegetable oil
1 cup chopped onions
1 green pepper, chopped
¼ pound mushrooms,
    sliced
½ teaspoon salt
¼ teaspoon dried ground
    red peppers

½ pound elbow macaroni,
    cooked and drained
1 10½-ounce can chili con
    carne
½ cup water
1 cup grated American
    cheese

Heat the oil in a skillet. Sauté the onions and green pepper 5 minutes. Add the mushrooms, salt, and red peppers. Sauté 5 minutes.

Spread half the macaroni in a buttered casserole. Spread the mushroom mixture over it. Combine the chili con carne and water and pour half into the casserole. Add the balance of macaroni and cover with the remaining chili con carne. Sprinkle with the cheese. Bake in a 350° oven 30 minutes.

Serves 4.

With Poultry

*P*OULTRY, particularly chicken, has always been considered both a staple and a party food. But plain chicken can become extremely monotonous. Combined with *pasta*, poultry becomes more versatile, as indicated by the number of foreign recipes incorporating *pasta* of one variety or another. Leftover poultry can also be used, thus making the eating of leftover turkey or chicken a delight rather than a tiresome necessity.

CHICKEN SOUFFLE

2 *tablespoons butter*	1 *cup julienne-cut cooked*
3 *tablespoons flour*	*chicken or turkey*
1 *cup light cream, scalded*	1 *cup sliced, sautéed*
1 *onion, peeled and sliced*	*mushrooms*
1 *bay leaf*	¼ *cup fine noodles, cooked*
1 *teaspoon salt*	*and drained*
½ *teaspoon freshly ground*	4 *egg whites*
black pepper	2 *tablespoons grated*
4 *egg yolks*	*Parmesan cheese*

Melt the butter in a skillet; blend in the flour. Gradually add the cream, stirring constantly to the boiling point. Add the onion, bay leaf, salt, and pepper and cook 5 minutes, stirring frequently. Strain.

Beat the egg yolks in a bowl until light. Add the hot sauce, beating constantly. Mix in the chicken, mushrooms, and noodles. Taste for seasoning. Let cool 10 minutes.

Beat the egg whites until stiff but not dry. Fold carefully into the chicken mixture. Pour into a buttered 2-quart soufflé dish. Sprinkle with the Parmesan cheese. Bake in a preheated 350° oven 35 minutes. Serve immediately, or the soufflé will fall.

Serves 4.

CHICKEN TETRAZZINI

6 tablespoons butter
2 tablespoons flour
2 cups chicken stock
½ teaspoon white pepper
1 cup heavy cream
2 tablespoons sherry
¼ cup grated Gruyère or
   Swiss cheese

¼ pound mushrooms, sliced
½ pound spaghetti, cooked
   and drained
2 cups finely sliced cooked
   chicken
½ cup grated Parmesan
   cheese

Melt half the butter in a skillet. Blend in the flour until smooth. Gradually add the stock, stirring constantly to the boiling point. Add the pepper, cream, sherry, and Gruyère cheese. Cook over low heat 10 minutes, stirring frequently. Correct seasoning if necessary.

Melt the remaining butter in a skillet. Sauté the mushrooms 5 minutes. Add the spaghetti and half the sauce. Mix lightly. Spread in a buttered 1½-quart casserole. Mix the chicken with remaining sauce and pour over the spaghetti. Sprinkle with Parmesan cheese. Bake in a 350° oven 30 minutes.

Serves 4–6.

BREAST OF CHICKEN WITH FOIE GRAS
(Suprêmes de Volaille Strasbourgeoise)

4 *tablespoons butter*	1 *small can* pâté de foie
2 *whole chicken breasts, cut*	gras
in half, boned, and	1¼ *cups cream*
skinned	¼ *pound thin spaghetti*
Salt	2 *truffles, sliced julienne*

Melt 3 tablespoons butter in a skillet and sauté the chicken breasts over medium heat until tender but not brown. Season lightly with salt; remove from skillet and keep hot.

Mix 2 tablespoons of the *pâté de foie gras* to a paste with 1 tablespoon cream. Add the rest of the cream to the skillet, bring to a boil, and season with salt. Add the creamed *foie gras* and blend in thoroughly. Dice the remaining *foie gras*.

Meanwhile cook the spaghetti in boiling salted water. Drain well and toss with the remaining butter, the diced *foie gras*, and the truffle slices (reserve 4 slices for garnish). Make a bed of the spaghetti on a heated platter and arrange the chicken breasts on top. Put a slice of truffle on each and pour the sauce over them.

Serves 4.

STUFFED CHICKEN

(Pollo Relleno)

3 teaspoons salt
1 teaspoon freshly ground
   black pepper
1 teaspoon paprika
2 cloves garlic, minced
6-pound roasting chicken
3 tablespoons olive oil
¾ cup grated onions
½ pound mushrooms, sliced

4 tablespoons dry bread
   crumbs
½ pound broad noodles,
   cooked and drained
2 pimientos, sliced
½ teaspoon basil
4 tablespoons melted
   butter

Mix 2 teaspoons salt, ½ teaspoon pepper, the paprika and garlic to a smooth paste. Rub into the chicken.

Heat the oil in a skillet; sauté the onions and mushrooms 5 minutes. Mix in the remaining salt and pepper, bread crumbs, noodles, pimientos, and basil. Stuff the chicken, fastening the opening with skewers or thread. (If there is too much stuffing, reserve it and heat in the pan just before serving.) Pour the melted butter over the chicken.

Roast in a 375° oven 2½ hours, or until chicken is tender. Baste frequently, adding water if pan becomes dry.

Serves 4–6.

MACARONI-STUFFED CHICKEN

4-pound pullet
6 cups water
1 stalk celery with leaves
1 onion
2½ teaspoons salt
4 tablespoons butter
2 tablespoons flour
½ cup light cream
¼ teaspoon freshly ground
    black pepper

⅛ teaspoon nutmeg
½ pound shell or elbow
    macaroni, cooked and
    drained
1 cup sliced, sautéed
    mushrooms
½ cup grated Parmesan
    cheese

Clean and wash the whole chicken. Place in a deep saucepan with the water, celery, onion, and 2 teaspoons salt. Bring to a boil; cover and cook over low heat 1½ hours, or until the chicken is tender. Drain chicken and keep hot. Strain and reserve 1 cup stock.

Melt the butter in a saucepan; blend in the flour. Add the stock and cream, stirring constantly to the boiling point. Stir in the pepper, nutmeg, and remaining salt; cook over low heat 5 minutes.

Toss the macaroni with half the sauce and the mushrooms. Stuff the chicken with the mixture and close the opening. Place breast side up in a buttered baking pan. Pour the remaining sauce on top. Bake in a 400° oven 10 minutes. Sprinkle with the cheese and bake 5 minutes longer, or until cheese is delicately browned.

Serves 4.

CHICKEN AND VERMICELLI STEW

4 tablespoons olive oil
4-pound chicken,
  disjointed
2 quarts boiling water
2 teaspoons salt
¼ teaspoon pepper
3 onions, chopped

2 green peppers, chopped
½ pound vermicelli, broken
  in half
1 cup sliced black olives
2 pimientos, chopped
1 cup Parmesan cheese

Heat the oil in a skillet. Add the chicken pieces and brown well on all sides. Transfer the chicken to a saucepan, reserving the oil in the skillet. Add the water, salt, and pepper to the chicken. Bring to a boil and cook over low heat 1½ hours, or until chicken is tender. Remove the chicken and cut meat off the bones. Reserve the stock.

Sauté the onions and green peppers in the reserved oil until browned. Bring the stock to a boil and add the vegetables and vermicelli. Cook over medium heat 8 minutes. Mix in the olives, pimientos, cheese, and chicken. Cook 3 minutes. Serve in deep plates with grated cheese.

Serves 6–8.

CHICKEN-SPAGHETTI CASSEROLE

2 tablespoons olive oil
¾ cup chopped onions
1 green pepper, chopped
1 cup sliced mushrooms
2 8-ounce cans tomato
  sauce
½ teaspoon orégano

½ teaspoon pepper
1 pound spaghetti, cooked
  and drained
2 cups diced, cooked
  poultry
½ pound mozzarella cheese,
  grated

Heat the olive oil in a skillet. Sauté the onions and green pepper

10 minutes. Add the mushrooms, tomato sauce, orégano, and pepper. Cook over low heat 30 minutes. Correct seasoning if necessary.

In a buttered casserole, arrange alternate layers of spaghetti, poultry, sauce, and cheese, ending with cheese. Bake in a 375° oven 35 minutes.

Serves 4–6.

SPANISH CHICKEN CASSEROLE

(Cazuela de Pollo y Tallerines)

1 *pound spaghetti, cooked and drained*

3 *cups diced, cooked chicken*

2 *cups cooked or canned corn kernels*

1 *cup canned green peas*

½ *pound mushrooms, sliced and sautéed*

2 *cups canned tomatoes, chopped*

1½ *teaspoons salt*

½ *teaspoon freshly ground black pepper*

½ *cup grated Parmesan cheese*

Mix together the spaghetti, chicken, corn, peas, mushrooms, tomatoes, salt, and pepper. Taste for seasoning and turn into a greased casserole; sprinkle with the cheese. Bake in a 350° oven 30 minutes, or until bubbly hot and browned.

Serves 6–8.

NOODLE CASSEROLE A LA REINE

6 tablespoons butter
½ cup chopped onions
¼ pound mushrooms,
 sliced
¼ cup chopped green
 pepper
2 tablespoons flour
1½ cups hot chicken broth
1½ cups light cream
2 egg yolks

1 teaspoon salt
¼ teaspoon freshly ground
 black pepper
¼ cup dry sherry
3 cups diced, cooked
 chicken
½ pound medium noodles,
 cooked and drained
½ cup grated Parmesan
 cheese

Melt 4 tablespoons butter in a skillet; sauté the onions, mushrooms, and green pepper 5 minutes, stirring frequently. Blend in
the flour; add the broth and cream, stirring steadily to the boiling
point, then cook over low heat 5 minutes.

Beat the egg yolks with the salt and pepper; gradually add the
hot sauce, stirring steadily to prevent curdling. Mix in the sherry,
chicken, and noodles. Taste for seasoning. Turn into a 2-quart
casserole; sprinkle with the cheese and dot with the remaining butter. Bake in a 350° oven 25 minutes, or until top is browned.
Serves 4–6.

HUNGARIAN CHICKEN AND NOODLES

3 tablespoons butter
½ cup chopped onions
½ pound uncooked fine
 noodles
2½ cups chicken broth
1 teaspoon salt
1 teaspoon paprika

1 cup sour cream
2 cups diced, cooked
 chicken
¼ cup slivered toasted
 almonds
2 tablespoons poppy seeds

Melt the butter in a saucepan; sauté the onions 5 minutes. Stir in the noodles, then add the broth and salt. Bring to a boil; cover and cook over low heat 15 minutes. Mix in the paprika, sour cream, and chicken. Taste for seasoning; heat. Serve sprinkled with the almonds and poppy seeds.

Serves 4.

CHINESE CHICKEN AND NOODLES

2 whole chicken breasts
4 tablespoons vegetable oil
1 cup thinly sliced onions
2 cups sliced celery
2 cups bean sprouts
1 teaspoon salt
¼ teaspoon freshly ground
    black pepper

2 tablespoons soy sauce
½ teaspoon sugar
1 tablespoon cornstarch
¾ cup chicken broth
½ pound fine noodles,
    cooked and drained

Remove and discard the skin and bones of the chicken; cut the chicken into narrow strips. Heat the oil in a deep skillet; sauté the chicken 5 minutes. Mix in the onions, celery, bean sprouts, salt, pepper, soy sauce, and sugar. Cover and cook over low heat 8 minutes. Mix together the cornstarch and broth; stir into the skillet until thickened. Add the noodles. Cook 2 minutes.

Serves 4.

CHINESE MINCED CHICKEN AND NOODLES

2 whole chicken breasts
½ teaspoon baking soda
½ cup vegetable oil
½ pound fine noodles,
    cooked, drained, and
    chilled
½ cup chopped green onions
2 teaspoons salt

¼ teaspoon freshly ground
    black pepper
½ teaspoon Ac'cent
1 clove garlic, minced
1 can bean sprouts, drained
4 cups finely shredded
    lettuce

Remove the skin and bones of the chicken and shred chicken finely. Toss with the baking soda.

Heat the oil in a skillet; fry the noodles until browned, stirring frequently. Drain and keep warm. Add the green onions to the oil remaining in the skillet; sauté 1 minute. Add the chicken; cook, mixing steadily, until chicken turns white. Mix in the salt, pepper, Ac'cent, garlic, and bean sprouts. Cook over low heat 5 minutes, stirring frequently.

Heap the lettuce on a serving dish and pour the chicken mixture over it. Cover with the fried noodles.

Serves 4–6.

BURMESE NOODLES AND CHICKEN

(Chet-Glay Ne Kaukswe)

1 cup packaged fine grated
  coconut
2 cups milk
3-pound fryer, disjointed
5 cups water
2 teaspoons salt
1 teaspoon saffron
2 cups chopped onions
2 cloves garlic, minced
½ teaspoon dried ground
  red peppers
2 teaspoons minced ginger
  root or 1 tablespoon
  powdered
¼ cup sesame or vegetable
  oil
1 tablespoon cornstarch
1 pound fine noodles,
  cooked and drained
Chopped green onions
Diced cucumbers

Rinse the coconut under cold running water. Add the milk, bring to a boil, and let stand 30 minutes. Strain, pressing out all the liquid. Discard the coconut.

Wash the chicken. Bring the water, salt, and saffron to a boil; add the chicken. Cover and cook over low heat 1 hour. Remove the chicken and cut into bite-sized pieces. Cook the stock over high heat until reduced to 2 cups.

Pound together the onions, garlic, red peppers, and ginger to a paste, then combine with the chicken, tossing until the pieces are coated.

Heat the oil in a skillet; brown the chicken pieces. Mix in the stock; cover and cook over low heat 15 minutes. Blend the cornstarch with a little of the coconut milk, then add to the skillet with all the coconut milk, stirring steadily to the boiling point, then cook 5 minutes longer. Divide the noodles among 4 to 6 bowls and pour the chicken mixture over them. Garnish with the green onions and cucumbers.

Serves 4–6.

CURRIED NOODLES AND CHICKEN, THAILAND STYLE

3 cups packaged fine grated coconut
4 cups milk
½ cup sesame oil or peanut oil
3 onions, chopped fine
6 cloves garlic, minced
1-inch piece fresh ginger, chopped fine, or 2 teaspoons powdered ginger
1 tablespoon curry powder
2 4-pound chickens, boned and cut into small cubes

1 cup boiling water
2 teaspoons salt
¼ cup cornstarch or potato flour
¼ cup cold water
1½ pounds broad noodles, cooked and drained
1 fresh chili pepper, chopped fine, or ½ teaspoon dried ground chili peppers
4 hard-cooked eggs, chopped
6 green onions, sliced thin

Rinse the coconut under cold running water, then combine with the milk in a saucepan. Bring to a boil; remove from the heat and let soak 30 minutes. Press all the liquid from the coconut. Reserve the coconut milk and discard the pulp.

Heat the oil in a saucepan. Sauté the onions, garlic, and ginger 10 minutes, stirring frequently. Stir in the curry powder. Add the cubed chicken and sauté 15 minutes, turning the pieces a few times. Add 2 cups of the coconut milk, the boiling water, and the salt. Cover and cook over low heat 30 minutes, or until the chicken is tender. Mix the cornstarch and water to a smooth paste.

Add to the chicken mixture, stirring constantly to the boiling point. Cook over medium heat 10 minutes, stirring frequently. Mix in the remaining coconut milk. Heat, but do not allow the mixture to boil.

Arrange the noodles on a large platter or divide into individual portions. Sprinkle with the chili peppers, eggs, and green oinons. Pour the chicken mixture on top and serve at once.

Serves 8–10.

SQUABS STUFFED WITH NOODLES

1 *pair sweetbreads*	½ *pound (2 sticks) butter*
1 *cup water*	1 *cup chopped onions*
1 *tablespoon vinegar*	1 *cup chopped mushrooms*
3 *teaspoons salt*	2 *cups medium egg*
1½ *teaspoons pepper*	*noodles, cooked and*
2 *cloves garlic, minced*	*drained*
6 *squabs, with livers and*	1 *cup heavy cream*
gizzards	¾ *cup dry sherry*

Wash the sweetbreads in cold water. Drain. Combine in a saucepan with 1 cup water and the vinegar. Bring to a boil and cook over low heat 10 minutes. Drain. Cover with cold water and let stand 20 minutes. Drain. Remove the membranes and cut the sweetbreads into small cubes. Mix 2 teaspoons salt, 1 teaspoon pepper, and the garlic to a smooth paste. Rub into the squabs. Grind the livers and gizzards in a food chopper.

Melt half the butter in a skillet; sauté the onions and mushrooms 5 minutes, stirring frequently. Add the ground giblets; sauté 5 minutes. Mix in the noodles, sweetbreads, cream, sherry, and remaining salt and pepper. Taste for seasoning. Stuff the squabs with the mixture, fastening the openings with skewers or thread.

Melt the remaining butter in a casserole or Dutch oven. Brown the squabs on all sides over direct heat, then roast in a 375° oven 35 minutes, or until tender. Baste frequently.

Serves 6.

NOODLES WITH DUCK
(Pappardelle coll' Anitra)

2 *cups sifted flour*	4 *tomatoes, chopped*
2½ *teaspoons salt*	½ *cup dry red wine*
2 *eggs*	½ *teaspoon pepper*
1 *egg yolk*	½ *teaspoon basil*
2 *tablespoons vegetable*	⅛ *teaspoon thyme*
oil	2 *tablespoons chopped*
5-*pound duck, disjointed*	*parsley*

Sift the flour and ½ teaspoon salt onto a board. Make a well in the center and place the eggs and egg yolk in it. Work in the flour until a dough is formed. Knead until smooth and elastic. Cover with a bowl and let stand 20 minutes. Roll out the dough as thin as possible. Let dry while preparing the duck. (If you don't want to prepare the noodles yourself, use ¾ pound broad egg noodles.)

Heat the oil in a skillet. Add the duck and brown lightly. Pour off the fat. Mix in the tomatoes. Cook over low heat 15 minutes. Add the wine, pepper, basil, thyme, parsley, and remaining salt. Cover and cook over low heat 1½ hours. Taste for seasoning.

Cut the dough into 2-inch squares. Boil in salted water 10 minutes. Drain. Add to sauce. Mix lightly and serve.

Serves 4–5.

SPAGHETTI WITH CHICKEN LIVERS

4 tablespoons butter
3 tablespoons olive oil
1 cup chopped onions
2 cloves garlic, minced
2 tablespoons chopped
  parsley
½ pound mushrooms, sliced
1 teaspoon salt
¼ teaspoon dried ground
  red peppers
½ teaspoon orégano

1 bay leaf
1 20-ounce can Italian-
  style tomatoes
1 can beef consommé
1 pound chicken livers,
  coarsely chopped
1½ cups grated Parmesan
  cheese
1 pound spaghetti,
  cooked and drained

Heat half the butter and all the olive oil in a skillet. Sauté the onions and garlic 10 minutes. Add the parsley, mushrooms, salt, red peppers, orégano, bay leaf, tomatoes, and consommé. Cook over low heat 2½ hours, stirring occasionally.

Sauté the livers in the remaining butter 5 minutes and add to the sauce. Cook 30 minutes. Add ½ cup cheese. Arrange the spaghetti in a ring on a platter. Pour half the sauce in the center and the balance over the spaghetti. Sprinkle with the remaining cheese.
Serves 4–6.

LINGUINI WITH CHICKEN-LIVER SAUCE

¼ cup olive oil
1 cup chopped onions
2 8-ounce cans tomato
  sauce
1½ teaspoons salt
¼ teaspoon dried ground
  red peppers

½ cup grated Parmesan
  cheese
4 tablespoons butter
1 pound chicken livers
½ pound mushrooms, sliced
1 pound linguini, cooked
  and drained

Heat the olive oil in a saucepan; sauté the onions 10 minutes.

Mix in the tomato sauce, ½ teaspoon salt, and the red peppers. Cook over low heat 15 minutes. Gradually stir in the cheese. Keep over very low heat while preparing the livers and mushrooms.

Melt the butter in a skillet; sauté the livers and mushrooms 5 minutes. Season with remaining salt. Combine with tomato sauce and cook 2 minutes. Taste for seasoning and pour over the spaghetti.

Serves 4.

CHICKEN-LIVER KREPLACH

3 *tablespoons butter or rendered chicken fat*	¼ *teaspoon freshly ground black pepper*
½ *pound chicken livers*	2 *cups sifted flour*
2 *hard-cooked eggs, chopped*	2 *eggs*
2 *teaspoons salt*	2 *tablespoons cold water*

Melt the butter in a skillet. Add the livers and sauté 10 minutes, stirring frequently. Chop or grind the livers. Mix in the hard-cooked eggs, 1½ teaspoons salt, and the pepper. Taste for seasoning. Cool.

Sift the flour and remaining salt onto a board. Make a well in the center, and into it put the eggs and water. Gradually work in the flour, kneading until a dough is formed. Continue kneading until smooth and elastic. Cover and let stand 20 minutes. Roll out the dough as thin as possible on a lightly floured surface. Cut into 2-inch squares. Place a teaspoonful of the liver mixture on each and fold over into triangles, sealing the edges carefully.

Drop into boiling salted water. Cook until they rise to the surface. Drain. The *kreplach* may be served in clear soup or as an accompaniment to main courses.

Serves 6–8.

CHICKEN-LIVER STUFFING

4 *tablespoons butter*	2 *tablespoons chopped*
1½ *cups chopped onions*	*parsley*
1 *clove garlic, minced*	¼ *pound macaroni,*
1 *cup chopped celery*	*cooked, drained, and*
¼ *pound mushrooms,*	*coarsely chopped*
sliced	1½ *teaspoons salt*
¼ *pound chicken livers,*	¼ *teaspoon pepper*
coarsely chopped	½ *teaspoon orégano*
	1 *egg, beaten*

Melt the butter in a skillet. Add the onions, garlic, and celery; sauté 10 minutes. Add the mushrooms and livers; sauté 5 minutes. Add the parsley, macaroni, salt, pepper, orégano, and egg. Mix lightly.

Makes enough to stuff a 5- to 6-pound bird. Double the recipe for a turkey.

NOODLE STUFFING

4 *tablespoons butter*	2 *eggs*
2 *cups chopped onions*	2 *teaspoons salt*
½ *pound medium noodles,*	½ *teaspoon pepper*
cooked and drained	3 *tablespoons chopped*
½ *cup dry bread crumbs*	*parsley*

Melt the butter in a skillet; sauté the onions 10 minutes. Combine with the noodles and bread crumbs. Beat the eggs with the salt, pepper, and parsley. Toss with the noodle mixture.

Makes enough to stuff a 5- to 6-pound bird. Double the recipe for a turkey.

CHEESE-NOODLE STUFFING

½ *pound bacon*
½ *cup grated onions*
½ *pound broad noodles,*
    cooked and drained
½ *teaspoon freshly ground*
    black pepper

½ *cup grated cheese*
2 *tablespoons chopped*
    pimiento
2 *eggs, beaten*

Fry the bacon until crisp. Drain, reserving 2 tablespoons of the fat. Sauté the onions in the fat 5 minutes, stirring frequently. Crumble the bacon and combine with the onions, noodles, pepper, cheese, pimiento, and eggs. Mix together well.

Makes enough to stuff a 5- to 7-pound chicken. Double the recipe for a turkey.

CHESTNUT-NOODLE STUFFING

1½ *pounds chestnuts,*
    cooked, peeled, and
    chopped
½ *pound fine noodles,*
    cooked and drained
3 *apples, peeled and diced*

2 *tablespoons grated*
    onion
2 *eggs, beaten*
¼ *cup melted butter*
1½ *teaspoons salt*
¼ *teaspoon pepper*

Mix the chestnuts, noodles, apples, onion, and eggs together. Add the melted butter, salt, and pepper. Mix together lightly.

Makes enough to stuff a 12-pound turkey. For a 6-pound chicken, use half the ingredients specified.

Accompaniments to Main Courses

Many plain broiled or boiled foods can be enlivened by the proper accompaniment, and few foods are more suitable for this than *pasta*. Noodles, as well as *pasta*, are ideal because they have a bland, pleasing taste which accompanies almost any food.

FRENCH-FRIED NOODLES

1 *quart vegetable oil*   ½ *pound fine egg noodles*

Heat the oil in a deep fryer or saucepan to 375°. Put 1 cup of uncooked noodles in a strainer and lower it into the oil slowly. Fry until golden brown. Drain. Repeat with remaining noodles. Serve with Chinese dishes or as a base or topping for other dishes. The noodles will keep fresh in a tightly closed jar 2–3 weeks.

HOMEMADE SAUTEED EGG BARLEY

2 *cups sifted flour*   2 *tablespoons butter*
1 *teaspoon salt*   4 *tablespoons grated onion*
2 *eggs*   1 *teaspoon paprika*

Sift the flour and ½ teaspoon salt onto a board. Make a well in the center and place the eggs in it. Work in the flour, kneading until a stiff dough is formed. Add a little more flour if necessary. Break off pieces of the dough and roll into long, pencil-thin strips.

Chop into very small pieces, about the size of rice. Place on a baking sheet and bake in a 275° oven 15 minutes, or until the pieces are dry.

Melt the butter in a skillet. Add the onion, egg barley, paprika, and remaining salt. Sauté until lightly browned. Add water barely to cover. Cook over low heat 15 minutes. Cover the skillet and bake in a 350° oven 15 minutes, or until tender. Serve as an accompaniment to meat dishes.

Serves 4.

NOTE: Uncooked homemade egg barley may be stored as long as 3 weeks in a tightly closed glass jar.

NOODLE DUMPLINGS

(Spaetzel)

2 cups sifted flour   ½ teaspoon salt
2 eggs   2 tablespoons cold water

Sift the flour onto a board. Make a well in the center and put the eggs, salt, and water into it. Work in the flour until a dough is formed. If too dry, add a little more water; if too wet, a little more flour. Knead on a lightly floured board until smooth and elastic. Divide the dough into six pieces and roll into pencil-thin strips. Cut into 1-inch pieces and drop into boiling salted water. Cook until they rise to the surface. Drain. Serve hot with gravy, meats, or buttered bread crumbs.

Serves 6–8.

SWEET AND SOUR NOODLES

4 tablespoons butter	1 pound medium noodles,
1½ cups chopped onions	cooked and drained
½ cup cider vinegar	3 tablespoons chopped
½ cup beef broth	parsley
3 tablespoons brown	
sugar	

Melt the butter in a skillet. Sauté the onions 10 minutes, stirring frequently. Add the vinegar, broth, and brown sugar. Cook over low heat 5 minutes.

Heap the noodles on a heated serving dish. Pour the sauce over them and sprinkle with parsley.

If desired, the noodles may be placed under the broiler to brown for 2 minutes.

Serves 4–6.

MACARONI PIE

(Pasticcio de Maccheroni)

2 cups flour	2 cups Tomato Sauce (see
1 teaspoon salt	recipe)
¾ cup shortening	1 cup grated Parmesan
1 egg, beaten	cheese
3 tablespoons cold water	3 tablespoons melted butter
¾ pound elbow macaroni,	
cooked and drained	

Sift the flour and salt into a bowl; cut in the shortening with a pastry blender or two knives. Add the egg mixed with the water and toss until a ball of dough is formed. Chill 1 hour.

Roll out the dough until thin and use ¾ of it to line an 11-inch pie plate. Fill with a mixture of the macaroni, Tomato Sauce, cheese, and butter. Cover with the remaining thinly rolled dough. Cut a few slits in the top. Bake in a preheated 400° oven 30 minutes, or until browned. Serve hot, cut into wedges.

Serves 4–6.

PLAIN NOODLE RING

⅓ cup melted butter   *½ pound noodles, cooked and drained*

Toss the butter with the noodles. Butter a 9-inch ring mold thoroughly. Pack the noodles into the mold and press down firmly with the back of a large spoon. Unmold carefully onto a platter or serving dish.

The center may be filled with creamed vegetables, chicken, or fish.

Serves 4.

NOODLE RING

½ pound cream cheese   *6-ounce package medium*
3 eggs   *noodles, cooked and*
2 tablespoons sugar   *drained*
1 teaspoon salt   *2 tablespoons dry bread*
                                 crumbs
                                3 tablespoons melted butter

Beat the cheese with the eggs, sugar, and salt. Fold in the noodles. Turn into a buttered 9-inch ring mold. Sprinkle with the bread crumbs and butter.

Bake in a 375° oven 40 minutes, or until browned. Unmold carefully.

Serves 4–6.

NOODLE PUFF RING

3 egg yolks
1 cup heavy cream
½ pound fine noodles,
   cooked and drained

⅓ cup grated Parmesan
   cheese
½ teaspoon salt
⅛ teaspoon pepper
3 egg whites, stiffly beaten

Beat the egg yolks until thick. Mix in the cream, noodles, cheese, salt, and pepper. Fold in the egg whites carefully but thoroughly. Pour into a well-buttered 8-inch ring mold. Place in a shallow pan of water. Bake in a preheated 350° oven 55 minutes.

To unmold, run a knife around the edge and tap the sides. Turn out onto a warmed platter. Serve as an accompaniment to main courses or fill the center with a vegetable, fish, or chicken mixture.

Serves 4–6.

ALMOND-MACARONI CASSEROLE

3 tablespoons butter
2 cups canned tomatoes
1 tablespoon grated
   onion
1 teaspoon salt
¼ teaspoon freshly ground
   pepper

¾ pound elbow macaroni,
   cooked and drained
1½ cups grated American
   cheese
1 cup chopped almonds

Combine the butter, tomatoes, onion, salt, and pepper in a skillet. Cook over low heat 5 minutes.

In a buttered casserole, arrange alternate layers of the macaroni, cheese, and almonds. Pour tomato sauce over all. Cover and bake in a 350° oven 30 minutes.

Serves 4–6.

NOODLES WITH ALMONDS

¼ pound butter
¾ cup chopped onions
½ cup sliced, blanched
   almonds
1 teaspoon lemon juice

1½ teaspoons salt
¼ teaspoon pepper
⅛ teaspoon nutmeg
1 pound medium noodles,
   cooked and drained

Melt the butter in a skillet; sauté the onions 10 minutes. Add the almonds and sauté 3 minutes. Mix in the lemon juice, salt, pepper, and nutmeg.

Heap the noodles on a hot platter and pour the sauce over them. Toss until well mixed.

Serves 4–6.

MACARONI, HUNGARIAN STYLE

3 tablespoons butter
3 tablespoons flour
1½ cups beef broth
1 teaspoon salt
¼ teaspoon freshly ground
   black pepper

1 bay leaf
2 tablespoons vinegar
¾ cup sour cream
1 pound elbow macaroni,
   cooked and drained

Melt the butter in a saucepan. Blend in the flour until smooth. Gradually add the broth, stirring constantly to the boiling point. Add the salt, pepper, and bay leaf. Cook over low heat 5 minutes. Discard the bay leaf. Mix in the vinegar and sour cream. Add the macaroni and mix together lightly. Cook over low heat 3 minutes.

Serves 4.

MACARONI WITH CAPER SAUCE

(Macaroni à la Madrid)

¼ *pound (1 stick) butter*
2 *teaspoons anchovy paste*
¼ *cup dry sherry*
½ *teaspoon salt*
½ *teaspoon pepper*
2 *tablespoons drained
   capers*

1 *teaspoon lemon juice*
1 *tablespoon chopped
   parsley*
1 *pound shell macaroni,
   cooked and drained*

Melt the butter in a saucepan. Blend in the anchovy paste. Add the sherry, salt, and pepper. Cook over low heat 10 minutes. Add the capers, lemon juice, and parsley. Pour over the macaroni and toss lightly.

Serves 4–6.

GREEN NOODLES, ROMAN STYLE

5 *quarts water*
1 *tablespoon olive oil*
1 *tablespoon salt*
1 *pound green noodles*
¼ *pound butter*
2 *cloves garlic, sliced thin*
2 *teaspoons basil*

4 *tablespoons chopped
   parsley*
½ *teaspoon freshly
   ground black pepper*
½ *cup grated Parmesan
   cheese*

Bring the water to an active boil in a large saucepan. Add the olive oil, salt, and noodles. Cook 12 minutes, or until the noodles are tender but firm. Drain very well.

Return the noodles to the saucepan. Add the butter, garlic, basil, parsley, and pepper. Toss lightly until the butter melts. Place in a hot serving dish and sprinkle with the cheese.

Serves 4–6.

BUCKWHEAT AND NOODLES

(Kasha Varnitchkes)

1 *cup kasha (buckwheat groats)*	⅓ *cup rendered chicken fat or butter*
1 *egg*	1 *cup chopped onions*
2 *teaspoons salt*	1 *pound bowknot noodles, cooked and drained*
2½ *cups boiling water*	¼ *teaspoon pepper*

Put the kasha in a saucepan; break the egg into it. Cook over low heat, stirring steadily until dry, browned, and every grain separate. Add 1 teaspoon salt and the boiling water. Cover and cook over low heat 20 minutes. Drain if any water remains.

Meanwhile heat the fat or butter in a skillet and brown the onions. Toss with the kasha, noodles, pepper, and remaining salt. Serve hot.

Serves 4–6.

NOODLE-RAISIN PUDDING

½ *cup seedless white raisins, chopped*	3 *eggs*
½ *cup chopped onions*	1 *pound medium noodles, cooked and drained*
4 *tablespoons butter*	

Soak the raisins in cold water 15 minutes. Drain.

Brown the onions in the butter. Cool for 15 minutes. Beat the eggs very well and stir in the noodles, raisins, and undrained browned onions. Turn into a buttered 8-inch-square pan. Bake in a 375° oven 40 minutes, or until browned. Cut into squares and serve hot with meat or poultry.

Serves 6–8.

With Vegetables

*P*ASTA with vegetables eliminates the need for a separate starch in the menu, thus replacing potatoes. Combinations of vegetables and *pasta* are appealing even to people who don't ordinarily like green vegetables. The stuffed vegetables can be served as a first or main course, not just as an accompaniment to other dishes.

SPAGHETTI WITH ARTICHOKE SAUCE

4 tablespoons butter
1½ cups chopped onions
3 tablespoons flour
2 cups beef broth
1 19-ounce can tomatoes,
    chopped
2 teaspoons salt
½ teaspoon freshly ground
    black pepper
1 teaspoon orégano

4 tablespoons olive oil
2 cloves garlic, minced
½ pound mushrooms
1 package frozen artichoke
    hearts, thawed
½ pound chicken livers
1 pound spaghetti, cooked
    and drained
½ cup grated Parmesan
    cheese

Melt the butter in a saucepan. Sauté the onions 10 minutes. Add flour, stirring until smooth and browned. Add the broth gradually, stirring constantly to the boiling point. Mix in the tomatoes, 1 teaspoon salt, ¼ teaspoon pepper, and the orégano. Cook over low heat 1 hour.

Heat the olive oil in a skillet. Add garlic, mushrooms, and artichokes. Sauté 5 minutes. Remove. Add the livers to the oil remaining in the skillet; sauté 10 minutes. Add remaining salt and pepper. Combine with sauce and artichoke mixture and cook 3 minutes.

Heap the spaghetti on a hot platter and pour the sauce over it. Sprinkle with cheese.

Serves 4–6.

MACARONI AND KIDNEY BEANS

1 *pound dried kidney beans*	1 *pound elbow macaroni, half cooked and drained*
¼ *cup olive oil*	
1 *onion, chopped*	2 *cups beef broth*
2 *cloves garlic*	¼ *teaspoon dried ground red peppers*
2½ *teaspoons salt*	

Wash the beans. Cover with water, bring to a boil, and let soak 1 hour. Drain.

Heat the oil in a saucepan; sauté the onion and garlic 5 minutes. Add the beans and water to cover. Cook over medium heat 1½ hours, or until beans are tender. Add 1½ teaspoons salt after 1 hour of cooking time. Drain. Add the macaroni, broth, red peppers, and remaining salt. Bring to a boil and cook over medium heat 10 minutes. Taste for seasoning. Serve in deep bowls with garlic toast and grated cheese.

Serves 8–10.

BROCCOLI AND MACARONI

1 *bunch broccoli or 2 packages frozen*	¼ *teaspoon dried ground red peppers*
4 *tablespoons olive oil*	½ *cup grated Parmesan cheese*
1 *clove garlic, minced*	
1 *pound shell macaroni, cooked and drained*	

Wash the fresh broccoli thoroughly. Separate into flowerets. Cook in boiling salted water 12 minutes. Drain. (For frozen broccoli, cook 1 minute less than package directs. Drain.)

Heat the oil in a skillet; sauté the garlic 2 minutes, stirring frequently. Add the broccoli, macaroni, and red peppers. Cook over low heat, stirring frequently, 5 minutes. Serve with the grated Parmesan cheese.

Serves 4–6.

BROWNED CABBAGE NOODLES

(Kraut Fleckerl)

1 tablespoon salt	½ teaspoon sugar
4 cups finely shredded cabbage	¼ teaspoon pepper
½ cup (1 stick) butter or rendered chicken fat	1 pound broad noodles, cooked and drained

Sprinkle the salt on the cabbage and let stand 20 minutes. Drain thoroughly.

Heat the butter or fat in a deep skillet. Mix in the cabbage, sugar, and pepper. Cook over very low heat 45 minutes, stirring frequently. Add the noodles, toss lightly, and cook 3 minutes.

Serves 6–8.

STUFFED EGGPLANT

3 small eggplants	1 tablespoon chopped parsley
3 tablespoons olive oil	3 egg yolks
1 tablespoon butter	3 tablespoons grated Parmesan cheese
1 tablespoon flour	½ pound fine noodles, cooked and drained
¾ cup milk	
2 teaspoons salt	
¼ teaspoon freshly ground black pepper	3 egg whites, stiffly beaten

Cut the eggplants in half lengthwise. Scoop out the pulp carefully, reserving the shells. Cube the eggplant pulp. Heat the olive oil in a skillet; sauté the eggplant pulp 10 minutes, stirring frequently.

Melt the butter in a saucepan. Blend in the flour until smooth. Gradually add the milk, stirring constantly to the boiling point. Stir in the salt, pepper, and parsley. Beat the egg yolks in a bowl; gradually add the white sauce, stirring constantly to prevent curdling. Fold in the cheese, sautéed eggplant, and noodles, then fold in the egg whites.

Fill the eggplant shells with the mixture. Arrange in a greased baking dish. Bake in a 375° oven 25 minutes, or until the mixture is set. Serve at once.

Serves 6.

EGGPLANT WITH MEAT-MACARONI STUFFING

2 medium eggplants
2½ teaspoons salt
2 tablespoons vegetable oil
¾ cup chopped onions
1 pound ground beef
2 cloves garlic, minced
½ teaspoon freshly ground black pepper
¾ teaspoon orégano
1½ cups cooked elbow macaroni
¾ cup grated Parmesan cheese
1 29-ounce can tomatoes, drained and chopped

Wash the eggplants and place in a baking pan. Add water to a depth of ¼ inch. Bake in a 400° oven 20 minutes. Let stand until cool enough to handle. Discard the stems and cut each eggplant in half lengthwise. Scoop out the pulp and chop; sprinkle cavities with 1 teaspoon salt. Turn upside down to drain.

Heat the oil in a skillet; sauté the onions 5 minutes. Add the meat; cook over high heat 5 minutes, stirring almost steadily. Mix in the garlic, pepper, orégano, chopped eggplant pulp, and remaining salt; cook over low heat 10 minutes. Mix half the meat mixture with the macaroni, ¼ cup cheese, and ¾ cup tomatoes. Taste for seasoning. Stuff the eggplant halves with the macaroni mixture. Spread the remaining tomatoes and meat mixture in a baking dish. Arrange eggplants over it and sprinkle with the remaining cheese. Bake in a 400° oven 20 minutes. Cut eggplants into serving-sized portions.

Serves 6–8.

SPAGHETTI WITH FENNEL

(Spaghetti e Finocchio)

12 *anchovies*
¼ *cup olive oil*
1½ *cups chopped onions*
3 *cups sliced finocchio*
½ *cup water*
¼ *cup pine nuts or slivered almonds*

¼ *teaspoon freshly ground black pepper*
1 *pound spaghetti, cooked and drained*
3 *tablespoons melted butter*

Soak the anchovies in water 1 hour. Drain and chop.

Heat the oil in a saucepan. Sauté the onions 10 minutes. Add the anchovies, finocchio, and water. Cook over low heat 10 minutes. Mix in the nuts and pepper. Cook 5 minutes.

Mix spaghetti and butter on a hot platter. Pour sauce over spaghetti and serve.

Serves 4–6.

KOHLRABI WITH NOODLES

4 tablespoons butter	1 tablespoon chopped dill
1½ cups chopped onions	¼ teaspoon thyme
6 kohlrabi, peeled and	1½ teaspoons salt
sliced thin	¼ teaspoon freshly ground
2 tablespoons flour	black pepper
1 cup beef broth	½ pound fine noodles,
3 tablespoons chopped	cooked and drained
parsley	1 cup sour cream

Melt the butter in a saucepan; sauté the onions and kohlrabi 10 minutes, stirring frequently. Blend the flour until browned. Gradually add the broth, stirring constantly to the boiling point.

Mix in the parsley, dill, thyme, salt, and pepper. Cover and cook over low heat 20 minutes. Add the noodles and sour cream. Mix together lightly. Cook 5 minutes longer.

Serves 4–6.

NOODLES WITH LENTILS

(Pasta e Lenticchie)

1 cup lentils	¼ teaspoon freshly ground
1½ cups peeled, diced	black pepper
potatoes	¼ teaspoon dried sage
½ pound tomatoes,	4 cups water
chopped	½ pound noodles (ditalini
½ cup chopped onions	or anellini, *if avail-*
2 tablespoons olive oil	*able*)
2 teaspoons salt	

Wash the lentils. Cover with water, bring to a boil, and let soak 1 hour. Drain. Add the potatoes, tomatoes, onions, oil, salt, pepper, sage, and the 4 cups of water. Bring to a boil and cook over low heat 1 hour, stirring occasionally. Mash ingredients lightly. Bring to an active boil and mix in the noodles. Cook over medium heat 12 minutes, or until noodles are tender. Taste for seasoning. Most of the liquid should be absorbed. Serve with grated cheese if desired.

Serves 4–6.

MACARONI WITH MUSHROOMS

½ cup olive oil
2 pounds mushrooms,
   sliced
1 clove garlic, minced
1 teaspoon salt
¼ teaspoon freshly ground
   black pepper

1 tablespoon chopped
   parsley
1 pound elbow macaroni,
   cooked and drained
½ cup grated Parmesan
   cheese

Heat the oil in a skillet. Sauté the mushrooms and garlic over very low heat 15 minutes, stirring occasionally. Mix in the salt, pepper, and parsley. Cook 5 minutes. Taste for seasoning.

Heap the macaroni on a hot platter and pour the mushroom mixture over it. Toss lightly. Serve with the grated Parmesan cheese.

Serves 4–6.

SPAGHETTI WITH MUSHROOMS, NAPLES STYLE

(Spaghetti con Fungi alla Napoletana)

1½ pounds mushrooms, cut
   in half
½ cup olive oil
2 cloves garlic, minced
1½ pounds tomatoes, diced

2 teaspoons salt
¾ teaspoon freshly ground
   black pepper
1 pound spaghetti, cooked
   and drained

Cook the mushrooms 3 minutes in water to cover. Drain well.

Heat the oil in a skillet; sauté the mushrooms, garlic, tomatoes, salt, and pepper 10 minutes, stirring frequently. Taste for seasoning.

Heap the spaghetti on a serving dish and pour the sauce over it. Toss lightly and serve at once.

Serves 4–6.

SPAGHETTI WITH CREAMED MUSHROOMS

2 *tablespoons butter*
2 *tablespoons olive oil*
½ *cup thinly sliced green onions*
1 *pound mushrooms, sliced*
1 *teaspoon salt*

½ *teaspoon freshly ground black pepper*
2 *tablespoons flour*
2 *cups heavy cream*
1 *pound spaghetti, cooked and drained*

Heat the butter and olive oil in a skillet; sauté the green onions 5 minutes, stirring frequently. Add the mushrooms, salt, and pepper; sauté 10 minutes, stirring frequently. Mix in the flour. Add the cream, stirring constantly to the boiling point. Cook over low heat 5 minutes. Taste for seasoning.

Pour the sauce over the spaghetti, toss lightly, and serve.

Serves 4–6.

VERMICELLI WITH MUSHROOMS

1 *cup water*
1½ *cups chopped onions*
4 *tablespoons butter*
1 *pound mushrooms, sliced*
1 *teaspoon salt*
½ *teaspoon pepper*

¼ *teaspoon nutmeg*
1 *cup heavy cream*
1 *pound vermicelli, cooked and drained*
½ *cup grated Parmesan cheese*

Combine the water and onions in a saucepan. Cook over high heat until water evaporates. Add the butter and sauté 5 minutes. Mix in the mushrooms and sauté 5 minutes. Stir in the salt, pepper, nutmeg, and cream. Bring to a boil and cook over low heat 5 minutes.

Pour the sauce over the vermicelli and toss lightly. Sprinkle with grated Parmesan cheese.

Serves 4–6.

SPAGHETTI WITH MUSHROOM SAUCE

½ cup olive oil
¾ cup chopped onions
2 cloves garlic, minced
1 green pepper, chopped
1 cup grated carrots
2 stalks celery, chopped
½ pound mushrooms, sliced

1 teaspoon salt
¼ teaspoon dried ground red peppers
1 29-ounce can tomatoes
1 pound spaghetti, cooked and drained

Heat the olive oil in a saucepan. Add the onions, garlic, green pepper, carrots, celery, and mushrooms; sauté 10 minutes, stirring frequently. Mix in the salt, red peppers, and tomatoes. Cover and cook over low heat 1 hour.

Pour the sauce over the spaghetti, toss lightly, and serve.

Serves 4–6.

SPAGHETTI ORTICA

½ cup olive oil
¾ pound mushrooms, coarsely chopped
1 teaspoon salt
1½ teaspoons pepper

2 teaspoons lemon juice
¼ cup chopped parsley
1 pound spaghetti, cooked and drained

Heat the olive oil in a skillet; sauté the mushrooms 5 minutes, stirring frequently. Mix in the salt, pepper, lemon juice, and parsley. Cook over low heat 5 minutes.

Heap the spaghetti on a hot platter. Pour the mushroom mixture over it and toss lightly. Serve at once.

Serves 4–6.

SPAGHETTI WITH ONION SAUCE

3 *tablespoons butter*
3 *tablespoons olive oil*
1 *pound small white onions,*
   peeled
1 *teaspoon salt*
1 *teaspoon freshly ground*
   black pepper

1 *teaspoon sugar*
2 *8-ounce cans tomato sauce*
1 *cup beef broth*
1 *pound spaghetti, cooked*
   and drained

Heat the butter and olive oil in a saucepan. Add the onions, salt, pepper, sugar, tomato sauce, and broth. Cover and cook over low heat 30 minutes, stirring occasionally. Taste for seasoning.

Heap the spaghetti on a hot platter. Pour the sauce over it and serve immediately.

Serves 4–6.

SPAGHETTI WITH PEAS

(Spaghetti alla Ghiotta)

3 *tablespoons butter*
2 *cups drained canned*
   green peas
1 *truffle, thinly sliced*
½ *teaspoon freshly ground*
   black pepper

1 *pound spaghetti, cooked*
   and drained
½ *cup grated Parmesan*
   cheese

Melt the butter in a saucepan; add the peas, truffle, and pepper. Cook over low heat 5 minutes. Add to the hot spaghetti with the cheese. Toss together lightly.

Serves 4–6.

NOODLES AND PEAS

2 pounds green peas,
    shelled, or 2 packages
    frozen
½ cup finely chopped
    onions
1 cup water
1½ teaspoons salt
1 pound broad noodles,
    half cooked and
    drained

2 cups beef broth
½ teaspoon freshly ground
    black pepper
3 tablespoons melted
    butter
½ cup grated Parmesan
    cheese

Combine the peas, onions, and water in a saucepan. Cook 8 minutes. Add the salt and cook 2 minutes longer. Drain. Add the noodles, broth, and pepper. Cook over medium heat 5 minutes. Drain and stir in the butter. Serve sprinkled with the cheese.
Serves 4–6.

BRAZILIAN SPAGHETTI

6 slices bacon, diced
1½ cups sliced onions
1 clove garlic, minced
1 cup chopped green
    peppers
1½ cups canned tomatoes
1½ teaspoons salt
¼ teaspoon dried ground
    red peppers

1 teaspoon sugar
½ pound spaghetti, cooked
    and drained
½ cup sliced pimiento-
    stuffed olives
1 cup grated Parmesan
    cheese

Fry the bacon in a skillet until crisp. Remove bacon, leaving about 2 tablespoons fat in the skillet. Add the onions; sauté 5 minutes. Add the garlic and green peppers; sauté 5 minutes. Mix in the tomatoes, salt, dried red peppers, and sugar. Cook over low heat 30 minutes. Add the spaghetti, olives, and ½ cup of cheese. Heat. Taste for seasoning.

Place on a heated platter and sprinkle the remaining cheese on top.

Serves 4.

SPAGHETTI WITH GREEN PEPPERS

¼ cup olive oil	¼ cup water
1½ cups thinly sliced onions	½ teaspoon freshly ground
5 green peppers, cut	black pepper
julienne	¼ pound bacon, diced
1½ pounds tomatoes, peeled	1 pound spaghetti, cooked
and diced	and drained

Heat the olive oil in a saucepan. Sauté the onions 10 minutes, stirring frequently. Add the green peppers, tomatoes, water, and black pepper. Cook over low heat 25 minutes, stirring frequently.

Half cook the bacon. Drain and add to the sauce. Cook over low heat 10 minutes, stirring occasionally. Taste for seasoning.

Pour over the spaghetti, toss lightly, and serve.

Serves 4–6.

PIMIENTO NOODLE RING

3 eggs	¼ teaspoon freshly ground
¾ cup heavy cream	black pepper
¼ cup chili sauce	1 teaspoon Worcestershire
⅓ cup grated Gruyère or	sauce
Swiss cheese	½ pound fine noodles,
4 pimientos, chopped	cooked and drained
1 teaspoon salt	

Beat the eggs in a bowl; mix in the cream, chili sauce, cheese, pimientos, salt, pepper, and Worcestershire sauce. Add the noodles and toss lightly but thoroughly.

Pour into a well-buttered 9-inch ring mold. Place the mold in a pan of hot water. Bake in a 350° oven 30 minutes, or until set. Run a knife around the edge and turn out carefully. If desired, the center may be filled with vegetables, meat, or poultry.

Serves 4.

POTATOES AND MACARONI

⅓ cup olive oil
3 onions, sliced
3 potatoes, peeled and
  diced
1 19-ounce can tomatoes
2 teaspoons salt
¼ teaspoon dried ground red
  peppers
¼ cup chopped parsley
½ cup grated Parmesan
  cheese
½ pound macaroni (shells
  or elbow macaroni),
  cooked and drained

Heat the olive oil in a saucepan. Sauté the onions 5 minutes, stirring frequently. Add the potatoes. Cook over medium heat until lightly browned. Mix in the tomatoes, salt, dried red peppers, and parsley. Cook over low heat 25 minutes, stirring occasionally. Add the cheese and macaroni. Toss together. Taste for seasoning.

Serves 4–6.

POTATO-STUFFED NOODLES

(Potato Pirogen)

2 pounds potatoes
2 cups sifted flour
2½ teaspoons salt
4 eggs
3 tablespoons ice water
¼ teaspoon freshly ground
  black pepper
2 tablespoons chopped
  parsley
¼ cup chopped green onions
½ cup melted butter

Cook the potatoes in their skins until tender. Drain, peel, and put through a ricer or mash very smooth.

Sift the flour and 1 teaspoon salt onto a board. Make a well in the center. Place 2 of the eggs and the ice water in it. Work in the flour, kneading until a soft dough is formed. Add a little more water or flour if necessary to make the dough. Let stand 15 minutes. Roll out the dough as thin as possible. Cut into 3-inch circles.

Beat the potatoes, remaining eggs and salt, the pepper, parsley, and green onions until very smooth and fluffy. Place a tablespoonful of the mixture on each circle. Fold over the dough, sealing the edges very carefully.

Drop into boiling salted water. Boil 10 minutes. Drain well. Serve with the melted butter.

Serves 6–8.

INDIAN RICE AND SPAGHETTI
(Bhat Aur Savia)

2 cups raw rice	1 teaspoon cinnamon
½ pound spaghetti	3 cloves
¼ pound (1 stick) butter	½ teaspoon cumin seeds
1½ cups chopped onions	2 teaspoons salt
1 clove garlic, minced	Boiling water

Wash the rice; let soak 30 minutes in warm water to cover. Drain. Break the spaghetti into 3-inch lengths.

Melt the butter in a saucepan; sauté the onions and garlic 5 minutes. Add the rice and spaghetti. Cook over low heat 5 minutes, stirring almost constantly. Mix in the cinnamon, cloves, cumin seeds, and salt. Add boiling water barely to cover. Cover the saucepan and cook over low heat until the water is absorbed and the rice is tender, about 15 minutes. Stir occasionally with a fork.

Serves 4–6.

NOODLES FLORENTINE

2 packages frozen chopped
    spinach, cooked and
    drained
4 tablespoons melted
    butter
1 tablespoon lemon juice
⅛ teaspoon nutmeg
Salt
1 pound noodles, cooked
    and drained

1 clove garlic, minced
¼ cup olive oil
¼ cup grated Gruyère or
    Swiss cheese
¼ teaspoon freshly ground
    black pepper
½ cup grated Parmesan
    cheese
2 tablespoons butter

Mix together the spinach, melted butter, lemon juice, nutmeg, and salt to taste. Spread in a buttered baking dish.

Toss together the noodles, garlic, oil, Gruyère cheese, and pepper. Spread over the spinach. Sprinkle with the Parmesan cheese and dot with the butter. Bake in a 475° oven 5 minutes.

Serves 4–6.

NOODLE-SPINACH PUDDING

4 egg yolks
4 tablespoons chopped
    green onions
2 cups cooked chopped
    spinach

½ pound fine noodles,
    cooked and drained
1 teaspoon salt
⅛ teaspoon nutmeg
4 egg whites, stiffly beaten

Beat the egg yolks, then stir in the green onions, spinach, noodles, salt, and nutmeg. Fold in the egg whites. Pour into a 1½-quart greased baking dish.

Bake in a 350° oven 30 minutes. Serve hot with meat or dairy dishes.

Serves 4–6.

CREOLE SPAGHETTI

¼ pound (1 stick) butter
1½ cups thinly sliced onions
1 clove garlic, minced
2 green peppers, thinly
   sliced
¼ pound mushrooms,
   sliced
1 16-ounce can tomatoes,
   strained
1 cup beef broth
1½ teaspoons salt

¼ teaspoon freshly ground
   pepper
⅛ teaspoon cayenne
   pepper
1 bay leaf
¾ cup sliced pimiento-
   stuffed olives
2 tablespoons dry sherry
1 pound spaghetti,
   cooked and drained

Melt the butter in a saucepan. Sauté the onions, garlic, and green peppers 5 minutes. Add the mushrooms and sauté 5 minutes. Mix in the tomatoes, broth, salt, pepper, cayenne pepper, and bay leaf. Cover and cook over low heat 30 minutes. Mix in the olives and sherry and cook 5 minutes longer. Discard the bay leaf and taste for seasoning.

Pour the sauce over the spaghetti and toss together lightly. *Serves 4.*

BAKED MACARONI

(Maccheroni al Forno)

¼ cup melted butter
¼ cup olive oil
1 pound macaroni, cooked
   and drained
6 tomatoes, peeled and
   sliced

2 teaspoons salt
¾ teaspoon freshly ground
   black pepper
1 cup grated Parmesan
   cheese

Combine the butter and olive oil. Rub a casserole with 2 tablespoons of the mixture.

Spread half the macaroni in the casserole. Arrange half the tomatoes on top and sprinkle with half the salt and pepper. Cover with half the remaining butter and olive oil mixture. Repeat the layers, using the remaining macaroni, tomatoes, salt, pepper, and butter and olive oil mixture. Bake in a 350° oven 20 minutes. Sprinkle with the grated cheese and bake 10 minutes longer.

Serves 4–6.

STUFFED TOMATOES

6 *large, firm tomatoes*	¼ *teaspoon freshly ground*
4 *tablespoons olive oil*	*black pepper*
¾ *cup chopped onions*	¼ *teaspoon basil*
¼ *pound ground beef*	½ *pound spaghetti, broken*
1 *teaspoon salt*	*into 1-inch pieces,*
	cooked and drained

Cut a ½-inch slice from the stem end of the tomatoes and reserve. Carefully scoop out the pulp and chop.

Heat the olive oil in a skillet. Sauté the onions and beef 5 minutes, stirring frequently. Mix in the tomato pulp, salt, pepper, and basil. Cook over low heat 10 minutes, stirring frequently. Mix in the spaghetti. Stuff the tomatoes with the mixture and cover with the reserved tops. Arrange in a buttered baking dish. Bake in a 350° oven 20 minutes, or until the tomatoes are tender.

Serves 6.

SPAGHETTI, SICILIAN STYLE
(Spaghetti alla Siciliana)

½ cup olive oil
2 cloves garlic, minced
2 cups peeled, diced
  zucchini
2 green peppers, cut into
  eighths
3 cups peeled, diced
  tomatoes or canned
  tomatoes
1 teaspoon salt

¼ teaspoon black pepper
½ teaspoon basil
2 tablespoons anchovy
  paste
1 tablespoon capers
½ cup sliced black olives
  (Italian or Greek, if
  possible)
1 pound spaghetti, cooked
  and drained

Heat the oil in a saucepan; sauté the garlic, zucchini, and green peppers 10 minutes. Add the tomatoes, salt, pepper, and basil. Cover and cook over low heat 30 minutes. Mix in the anchovy paste, capers, and olives; re-cover and cook 10 minutes longer. Pour over the hot, drained spaghetti.

Serves 4–6.

ZUCCHINI WITH SPAGHETTI

½ cup olive oil
1 cup chopped onions
2 cloves garlic, minced
1 pound zucchini, thinly
  sliced
2 green peppers, cut
  julienne

4 tomatoes, chopped
3 tablespoons water
2 teaspoons salt
⅛ teaspoon dried ground
  red peppers
1 pound spaghetti, cooked
  and drained

Heat the olive oil in a skillet. Add onions, garlic, zucchini, and green peppers. Sauté 15 minutes, stirring occasionally. Mix in the tomatoes, water, salt, and red peppers. Cook over low heat 15 minutes. Add spaghetti, mixing lightly. Taste for seasoning.

Serves 4–6.

MACARONI WITH MUSHROOM-SOUR CREAM SAUCE

3 tablespoons butter
1½ cups chopped onions
1 green pepper, chopped
¼ pound mushrooms,
    chopped
1 19-ounce can tomatoes

1½ teaspoons salt
1 tablespoon sugar
1 cup sour cream, scalded
1 pound macaroni, cooked
    and drained

Melt the butter in a saucepan. Add onions, green pepper, and mushrooms; sauté 10 minutes. Mix in the tomatoes, salt, and sugar. Cook over low heat 1 hour. Blend in the sour cream. Cook 5 minutes. Taste for seasoning.

Heap the macaroni on a hot platter and pour sauce over it. *Serves 4–6.*

MACARONI A LA KING

¼ pound (1 stick) butter
⅓ cup sifted flour
3 cups milk
2½ teaspoons salt
¾ teaspoon pepper
½ teaspoon dry mustard
¾ pound mushrooms,
    sliced

2 green peppers, cut
    julienne
2 pimientos, diced
1 pound macaroni, cooked
    and drained
¼ cup ground nuts
¼ cup bread crumbs

Melt half the butter in a saucepan. Blend in the flour; gradually add the milk, stirring constantly to the boiling point. Add 1½ teaspoons salt, ¼ teaspoon pepper, and the mustard. Cook over low heat 5 minutes, stirring frequently.

Melt 2 tablespoons butter in a skillet; sauté the mushrooms and green peppers 10 minutes. Mix in the pimientos and the remaining salt and pepper.

Combine the white sauce, mushroom mixture, and macaroni in a buttered casserole. Sprinkle with nuts and bread crumbs and dot with the remaining butter. Bake in a 350° oven 30 minutes. *Serves 4–6.*

MACARONI LOAF

½ *pound macaroni, cooked
    and drained*
¼ *cup grated onion*
2 *tablespoons chopped
    parsley*
2 *pimientos, chopped*
1 *cup soft bread crumbs*

½ *cup melted butter*
1 *cup grated Gruyère or
    Swiss cheese*
2 *eggs*
1 *cup light cream*
1 *teaspoon salt*

Spread the macaroni in a buttered oblong baking dish. Sprinkle with the onion, parsley, and pimientos. Spread the bread crumbs on top, then sprinkle with the melted butter and cheese.

Beat the eggs in a bowl; mix in the cream and salt. Pour over the macaroni and cheese.

Bake in a 350° oven 30 minutes, or until set. *Serves 2–4.*

SPAGHETTI WITH VEGETARIAN MEAT BALLS

4 *tablespoons olive oil*
½ *pound mushrooms, sliced*
3 *cups chopped onions*
1 *29-ounce can tomatoes*
1 *6-ounce can tomato paste*
½ *teaspoon orégano*
1 *stalk celery, chopped*
3 *carrots, grated*
6 *tablespoons butter*

3 *eggs, beaten*
1½ *cups cracker meal*
2 *cups cooked green peas*
1 *teaspoon salt*
¼ *teaspoon pepper*
1 *pound spaghetti, cooked
    and drained*
Grated Swiss cheese

Heat the oil in a saucepan; sauté the mushrooms and 2 cups onions 10 minutes. Add the tomatoes, tomato paste, and orégano. Cover and cook over low heat 1 hour. Correct seasoning if necessary.

Cook the celery, carrots, and remaining onions in 3 tablespoons butter 15 minutes. Cool. Add the eggs, 1 cup cracker meal, the peas, salt, and pepper. Form into walnut-sized balls and dip in remaining cracker meal. Fry in the remaining butter until browned. Arrange over the spaghetti and pour the sauce over all. Serve with the grated Swiss cheese.

Serves 6.

SPAGHETTI WITH HERB SAUCE

3 *tablespoons fresh basil or*	1 *pound spaghetti, cooked*
2 *teaspoons dried*	*and drained*
½ *cup chopped parsley*	4 *tablespoons melted*
1 *clove garlic, minced*	*butter*
½ *cup olive oil*	½ *cup grated Parmesan*
	cheese

If dried basil is used, soak it in warm water 10 minutes. Drain very well. Combine the fresh or dried basil with the parsley and garlic and pound or mince very fine. Gradually add the olive oil, mixing constantly.

Pour over the spaghetti, tossing lightly. Add the melted butter and cheese and again toss lightly.

Serves 4–6.

SPAGHETTI NICOISE

¼ *cup olive oil*
3 *tablespoons butter*
¾ *cup thinly sliced onions*
1 *clove garlic, minced*
2 *carrots, grated*
½ *cup chopped parsley*
2 *cups tomato juice*
1 *teaspoon salt*

¼ *teaspoon freshly ground*
  black pepper
½ *pound mushrooms, sliced*
1 *pimiento, chopped*
½ *cup chopped black olives*
1 *pound spaghetti, cooked*
  and drained
1 *cup grated Parmesan*
  cheese

Heat the olive oil and butter in a skillet; sauté the onions, garlic, carrots, and parsley 10 minutes, stirring frequently. Add the tomato juice, salt, pepper, and mushrooms. Bring to a boil and cook over low heat 20 minutes. Taste for seasoning. Add the pimiento and olives. Pour over the spaghetti, toss lightly, and serve with the grated cheese.

Serves 4–6.

NOODLES WITH CHINESE VEGETABLES

5 *dried mushrooms*
½ *cup hot water*
⅓ *cup peanut or vegetable*
  oil
½ *cup sliced bamboo shoots*
¼ *pound spinach, washed,*
  drained, and chopped

1 *teaspoon salt*
1 *pound fine noodles,*
  cooked and drained
1 *tablespoon cornstarch*
2 *tablespoons soy sauce*
½ *teaspoon coarsely ground*
  black pepper

Wash the mushrooms and soak them in the hot water 10 minutes. Drain, reserving the liquid. Slice the mushrooms.

Heat the oil in a skillet. Add the bamboo shoots and mushrooms and sauté 3 minutes. Mix in the spinach and salt. Cook over high heat 1 minute, stirring constantly. Add the noodles and cook 3 minutes longer, again stirring constantly.

Mix the cornstarch and soy sauce to a smooth paste. Add the reserved mushroom liquid and pour the mixture over the noodles, stirring constantly to the boiling point. Cook over low heat 3 minutes. Sprinkle with pepper and serve.

Serves 4–6.

In Salads

SALADS made with *pasta* should be served as a separate course, as they are not meant to replace a green or vegetable salad. They make wonderful luncheon or supper dishes, particularly in the summer months. Be sure the *pasta* used in the recipe is very well drained and cooled before combining it with other ingredients.

SHRIMP AND MACARONI SALAD

¾ cup olive or vegetable oil
¼ cup wine vinegar
¾ teaspoon salt
¼ teaspoon freshly ground
   black pepper
1 clove garlic, minced
½ pound elbow macaroni,
   cooked, drained, and
   cooled

1 pound shrimp, cooked,
   shelled, and deveined
½ cup diced celery
½ cup julienne-cut green
   pepper
1 tomato, cut in wedges

Prepare a dressing with the oil, vinegar, salt, pepper, and garlic. In a bowl, toss together lightly the macaroni, shrimp, celery, and green pepper. Chill. Just before serving, add the tomato and dressing. Toss lightly.

Serves 4.

SALMON-MACARONI SALAD

2 7-ounce cans salmon,
  drained and flaked
2 tablespoons grated onion
1 cucumber, peeled and
  diced
1 green pepper, chopped
2 stalks celery, sliced
½ pound elbow macaroni,
  cooked, drained,
  chopped, and chilled

1 teaspoon salt
½ teaspoon freshly ground
  black pepper
1 cup mayonnaise
2 tomatoes, cut into
  eighths
3 hard-cooked eggs,
  quartered

Combine the salmon, onion, cucumber, green pepper, celery, macaroni, salt, pepper, and mayonnaise in a bowl. Toss lightly. Arrange the tomatoes and eggs around it. Serve cold.

Serves 4–6.

MACARONI-HAM SALAD

½ pound thinly sliced
  cooked ham
6 hard-cooked eggs
1 teaspoon salt
¼ teaspoon freshly ground
  black pepper
3 tablespoons mayonnaise
1 tablespoon prepared
  mustard

½ cup olive or vegetable
  oil
¼ cup vinegar
½ teaspoon dry mustard
2 tablespoons grated onion
½ pound shell or elbow
  macaroni, cooked,
  drained, and cooled
¼ cup chopped pimiento
Lettuce

Form each slice of ham into a cylinder. Cut the eggs in half; scoop out and mash the yolks. Mix in ½ teaspoon salt, ⅛ teaspoon pepper, the mayonnaise and prepared mustard. Stuff the whites.

Prepare a dressing with the oil, vinegar, dry mustard, onion, and remaining salt and pepper. Combine the macaroni and pimiento in a bowl; toss lightly with the dressing. Heap into 6 mounds on a bed of lettuce; arrange the ham rolls and stuffed eggs around each mound.

Serves 6.

MACARONI AND BACON SALAD

½ *cup olive oil*	8 *slices well-cooked bacon,*
2 *tablespoons wine vinegar*	*crumbled*
½ *teaspoon salt*	2 *tablespoons grated*
¼ *teaspoon freshly ground*	*onions*
black pepper	½ *cup mayonnaise*
2 *tablespoons ketchup*	3 *tomatoes, cut into*
1 *teaspoon capers, drained*	*eighths*
½ *pound elbow macaroni,*	3 *hard-cooked eggs,*
cooked, drained, and	*quartered*
cooled	

Beat together the olive oil, vinegar, salt, pepper, and ketchup. Add the capers.

Combine the macaroni, bacon, onions, and mayonnaise in a salad bowl, tossing lightly. Arrange the tomatoes and eggs around it. Pour the dressing over all.

Serves 4.

CHICKEN-MACARONI SALAD

2 *cups diced, cooked*	¼ *cup sour cream*
chicken	1½ *teaspoons salt*
1 *green pepper, chopped*	¼ *teaspoon freshly ground*
1 *cucumber, diced*	*black pepper*
1 *tablespoon grated onion*	¼ *pound macaroni,*
1 *pimiento, sliced*	*cooked and drained*
¾ *cup mayonnaise*	

Combine the chicken, green pepper, cucumber, onion, and pimiento in a bowl. Mix together the mayonnaise, sour cream, salt, and pepper. Pour over the chicken. Add the macaroni and toss lightly.

Serve on a bed of lettuce leaves.

Serves 2–4.

MACARONI AND BEAN SALAD

1 cup dried kidney beans or
    2 cups canned, drained
6 spicy sausages (Italian,
    if available)
2 onions, sliced thin (red,
    if available)
1 green pepper, cut julienne
2 tablespoons chopped
    parsley
½ pound elbow macaroni,
    cooked and drained

3 hard-cooked eggs,
    quartered
½ cup olive oil
3 tablespoons wine
    vinegar
1 clove garlic, minced
½ teaspoon salt
¼ teaspoon freshly ground
    black pepper
⅛ teaspoon orégano

If dried beans are used, soak overnight in water to cover. Drain, add fresh water to cover, and cook over medium heat 1½ hours. Add 1½ teaspoons salt after 1 hour. Drain and cool. It is not necessary to cook the canned beans.

Slice the sausages into 1-inch pieces. Fry until browned. Drain.

Combine the onions, green pepper, parsley, macaroni, eggs, beans, and sausages in a salad bowl. Toss lightly.

Beat together the oil, vinegar, garlic, salt, pepper, and orégano. Pour over the salad. Mix lightly.

Serves 4–6.

KIDNEY BEAN SALAD

1 1-pound can red kidney
   beans, drained
2 cups cooked shell
   macaroni

6 hard-cooked eggs, diced
⅓ cup pickle relish
½ cup mayonnaise
¼ cup French dressing

Combine the beans, macaroni, eggs, and pickle relish in a salad bowl. Mix together the mayonnaise and French dressing; pour over the ingredients in the bowl. Toss well. Chill. Serve on lettuce. *Serves 6.*

JELLIED TOMATO SALAD

4 cups tomato juice
2 teaspoons salt
¼ teaspoon freshly ground
   black pepper
¼ teaspoon basil
1 onion
2 envelopes (tablespoons)
   gelatin

¼ cup cold water
2 teaspoons prepared horseradish
2 teaspoons sugar
2 tablespoons lemon juice
¼ pound elbow macaroni,
   cooked and drained

Combine the tomato juice, salt, pepper, basil, and onion in a saucepan. Bring to a boil and cook over low heat 10 minutes. Strain.

Sprinkle the gelatin into the cold water and let stand 5 minutes. Add to the hot tomato juice, stirring until dissolved. Mix in the horseradish, sugar, and lemon juice. Chill until mixture begins to thicken. Add the macaroni. Pour mixture into a greased 9-inch ring mold. Chill until firm.

Carefully unmold. Fill center with any fish, vegetable, or meat salad.

Serves 4–6.

CORN SALAD

2 cups cooked or canned
    corn kernels
2 green peppers, chopped
3 pimientos, cut julienne
3 stalks celery, diced
3 tablespoons grated onion

½ pound spaghetti, cooked,
    drained, and chopped
¾ cup olive oil
3 tablespoons vinegar
1 teaspoon salt
¼ teaspoon pepper
¼ teaspoon paprika

In a salad bowl, mix together the corn, green peppers, pimientos, celery, onion, and spaghetti. Toss lightly.

Combine the olive oil, vinegar, salt, pepper, and paprika. Beat or shake very well. Pour over the salad just before serving.

Serves 4–6.

COTTAGE CHEESE AND MACARONI SALAD

1 pound cottage cheese
1 cup sour cream
2 tablespoons mayonnaise
2 teaspoons salt
¼ teaspoon pepper

2 tablespoons chopped
    chives or green onions
2 tomatoes, cubed
½ pound elbow macaroni,
    cooked and drained

Mix the cheese, sour cream, mayonnaise, salt, and pepper until smooth. Add the chives, tomatoes, and macaroni; toss together lightly. Serve on lettuce leaves.

Serves 4.

Sauces for Pasta

*T*HE sauces in this section can be used with any kind of *pasta*, ranging from plain spaghetti to elaborate *lasagne* preparations. They can also be used with plain meat or poultry, if you prefer. Sauces freeze perfectly, so when preparing a sauce recipe, double or triple the amount and store some in the freezer. The next time you want to serve a sauce, just heat it from the frozen state.

TOMATO SAUCE I

(Salsa di Pomodoro)

4 tablespoons butter	2 pounds very ripe toma-
½ cup chopped onions	toes, chopped
¼ cup grated carrots	2 teaspoons salt
¼ cup chopped celery	½ teaspoon freshly ground
2 tablespoons minced	black pepper
parsley	⅛ teaspoon sugar
	½ teaspoon basil

Melt the butter in a saucepan; sauté the onions, carrots, celery, and parsley 5 minutes. Add the tomatoes, salt, pepper, sugar, and basil. Bring to a boil and cook over low heat 45 minutes. Purée in an electric blender or force through a sieve. Use as directed in recipes, or serve as is with *pasta*.

Makes about 2½ cups.

TOMATO SAUCE II

(Salsa di Pomodoro)

¼ cup olive oil
1½ cups chopped onions
2 cloves garlic, minced
1 stalk celery, chopped
2 tablespoons chopped
  parsley
1 29-ounce can Italian-
  style tomatoes
1 6-ounce can tomato
  paste

1 teaspoon salt
½ teaspoon dried ground
  red peppers
1 tablespoon basil
1 bay leaf
½ pound mushrooms,
  chopped
¼ pound spinach, chopped
2 tablespoons dry white
  wine

Heat the oil in a saucepan. Add the onions, garlic, celery, and parsley; sauté 10 minutes. Mix in the tomatoes, tomato paste, salt, red peppers, basil, and bay leaf. Cook over low heat 3 hours, adding water if sauce becomes too thick. Mix in the mushrooms, spinach, and wine. Cook 30 minutes longer. Taste for seasoning. Serve with any *pasta*.

Makes about 2½ cups.

MUSHROOM SAUCE

2 tablespoons butter
2 tablespoons olive oil
½ cup thinly sliced green
  onions
1 pound mushrooms,
  sliced

1 teaspoon salt
½ teaspoon pepper
2 tablespoons flour
2 cups heavy cream

Heat the butter and olive oil in a skillet. Sauté the green onions 5 minutes. Add the mushrooms, salt, and pepper. Sauté 10 minutes, stirring frequently. Blend in the flour. Add the cream gradually, stirring constantly to the boiling point. Cook over low heat 5 minutes. Taste for seasoning.

Makes about 3 cups.

MARINARA SAUCE

½ cup olive oil
2 cloves garlic, minced
2 pounds tomatoes, peeled
 and chopped

3 tablespoons chopped
 parsley
1½ teaspoons salt
½ teaspoon pepper
½ teaspoon orégano

Heat the oil in a saucepan. Sauté the garlic 5 minutes. Add the tomatoes, parsley, salt, pepper, and orégano. Cook over very low heat 30 minutes. Taste for seasoning. For a very smooth sauce, purée the mixture in an electric blender. Serve with any *pasta*.

Makes about 2½ cups.

SICILIAN SAUCE

½ cup olive oil
¾ cup chopped onions
2 cloves garlic, minced
2 green peppers, cut
 julienne
2 pounds tomatoes, peeled
 and chopped, or 1 29-
 ounce can tomatoes

1 medium eggplant,
 peeled and diced
¾ cup sliced black olives
 (Italian or Greek)
1 tablespoon capers
1 teaspoon basil
4 anchovies, mashed
¼ teaspoon dried ground
 red peppers

Heat the oil in a skillet. Add onions, garlic, and green peppers; sauté 10 minutes. Mix in the tomatoes and eggplant gently; cook over low heat 30 minutes, stirring frequently. Add olives, capers, basil, anchovies, and red peppers. Cover and cook over low heat 10 minutes. Taste for seasoning. Serve with any *pasta*.

Makes about 4 cups.

CRAB MEAT SAUCE

¼ cup olive oil
1 cup chopped onions
1 clove garlic, minced
1 green pepper, chopped
1 29-ounce can tomatoes

¼ teaspoon dried ground
   red peppers
½ teaspoon basil
¾ pound crab meat

Heat the oil in a saucepan; sauté the onions, garlic, and green pepper 10 minutes. Add the tomatoes, red peppers, and basil. Bring to a boil and cook over low heat 30 minutes, stirring frequently. Carefully stir in the crab meat. Cook 3 minutes. Taste for seasoning and serve over any *pasta*.

Makes about 3 cups.

NEAPOLITAN SAUCE

2 tablespoons olive oil
1 pound boneless pork,
   cut into ½-inch cubes
¾ cup finely chopped onion
2 tablespoons minced
   parsley

2 cloves garlic, minced
2 6-ounce cans tomato
   paste
3½ cups water
1 teaspoon salt
½ teaspoon pepper

Heat the olive oil in a saucepan. Add the pork, onion, and parsley; sauté 15 minutes, mixing occasionally. Mix in the garlic, tomato paste, water, salt, and pepper. Cover and cook over low heat 2½ hours. Stir frequently and add water if sauce becomes too thick. Taste for seasoning. Serve with any *pasta*.

Makes about 3 cups.

BACON SAUCE

½ *pound bacon, diced*
2 *cloves garlic, minced*
1 *teaspoon crushed black peppercorns*

½ *cup grated Parmesan cheese*

Combine the bacon and garlic in a skillet. Fry until bacon is crisp. Stir in the pepper. Remove from heat and mix in the cheese. *Enough for 1 pound pasta.*

BROWN SAUCE

(Tocco alla Genovese)

6 *dried mushrooms (Italian, if available)*
¼ *cup olive oil*
2 *pounds chuck or rump of beef*
¾ *cup chopped onions*
2 *cloves garlic, minced*
½ *cup chopped celery*
½ *cup grated carrots*

2 *teaspoons salt*
½ *teaspoon freshly ground black pepper*
2 *bay leaves*
1 *cup dry red wine*
1 *6-ounce can tomato paste*
3 *cups hot beef broth*

Wash the mushrooms; cover with warm water and let soak 15 minutes. Drain and chop.

Heat the oil in a heavy saucepan; brown the meat on all sides over high heat. Reduce heat; add the onions, garlic, celery, and carrots. Cook until browned. Mix in the mushrooms, salt, and pepper; cook 5 minutes. Add the bay leaves and wine and bring to a boil. Stir in the tomato paste mixed with 2 cups of the broth. Cover and cook over low heat 2½ hours, adding some of the remaining broth from time to time. Taste for seasoning.

Discard the bay leaves and remove the meat. Serve the meat separately, and the sauce on any *pasta*.

Makes enough sauce for 1–1½ pounds pasta.

CHICKEN-LIVER SAUCE

(Salsa di Fegatini)

5 *dried mushrooms*	⅓ *cup Marsala or sweet*
1 *pound chicken livers*	*sherry*
3 *tablespoons flour*	1½ *cups chicken broth*
4 *tablespoons butter*	2 *tablespoons minced*
1 *teaspoon salt*	*parsley*
¼ *teaspoon freshly ground*	
black pepper	

Wash the mushrooms; cover with warm water and let soak 15 minutes. Drain and chop.

Wash the livers, remove any discolored areas, and dry. Dice the livers and toss with the flour.

Melt the butter in a saucepan; sauté the livers and mushrooms 5 minutes. Season with the salt and pepper and add the wine; cook over medium heat 3 minutes. Add the broth; cook over low heat 20 minutes. Mix in the parsley and taste for seasoning. Serve with any *pasta*, but particularly good with *gnocchi*.

Makes about 2½ cups.

SAUSAGE SAUCE, CALABRIA STYLE

(Salsa Salsiccia alla Calabria)

1 *pound sweet or hot Italian sausages, sliced*	1 *tablespoon chopped parsley*
2 *tablespoons water*	1 *16-ounce can Italian-style tomatoes*
1 *cup chopped onions*	
½ *cup finely chopped celery*	2 *8-ounce cans tomato sauce*
	2 *bay leaves*

Place the sausages and water in a saucepan; cook until the sausages begin to fry. Add the onions, celery, and parsley and cook until the sausages brown, stirring frequently. Add the tomatoes, tomato sauce, and bay leaves; cover and cook over low heat 1 hour, stirring occasionally. Uncover and cook 10 minutes. Remove the bay leaves and taste for seasoning. Serve on all *pasta*.

Makes about 4 cups.

TOMATO-MEAT SAUCE

(Sugo di Carne al Tomate)

2 *tablespoons olive oil*	1 *teaspoon basil*
½ *pound ground beef*	½ *teaspoon salt*
½ *pound ground pork*	¼ *teaspoon dried ground red peppers*
1 *cup chopped onions*	
1 *clove garlic, minced*	2 *tablespoons chopped parsley*
1 *29-ounce can tomatoes*	
1 *6-ounce can tomato paste*	2 *tablespoons butter*
2 *bay leaves*	

Heat the olive oil in a saucepan. Add the beef, pork, onions, and garlic. Cook over high heat, stirring constantly, until meat browns. Mix in the tomatoes, tomato paste, bay leaves, basil, salt, and peppers. Cover and cook over low heat 1½ hours, adding water if sauce becomes too thick. Taste for seasoning. Stir in the parsley and butter. Serve with any *pasta*.

Makes about 4 cups.

MEAT SAUCE (WITH WHITE WINE)
(Sugo di Carne)

3 *dried mushrooms*	1 *tablespoon flour*
2 *tablespoons butter*	1½ *teaspoons salt*
¾ *cup chopped onions*	½ *teaspoon freshly ground*
½ *cup grated carrots*	*black pepper*
3 *tablespoons minced*	2 *teaspoons tomato paste*
parsley	½ *cup dry white wine*
¾ *pound ground beef*	2 *cups beef broth*

Wash the mushrooms; cover with water and let soak 15 minutes. Drain and slice fine.

Melt the butter in a saucepan; sauté the onions, carrots, and parsley 5 minutes. Add the meat and mushrooms; cook over medium heat, stirring almost constantly until browned. Blend in the flour, salt, and pepper, then the tomato paste. Add the wine and broth. Cook over low heat 45 minutes, stirring frequently. Taste for seasoning. Serve with any *pasta*.

Makes about 3 cups.

MEAT SAUCE (WITH RED WINE)

1 *pound ground beef*
2 *tablespoons flour*
4 *tablespoons olive oil*
¾ *cup chopped onions*
¼ *cup grated carrots*
1 *tablespoon minced*
　parsley
¾ *cup dry red wine*

1½ *cups canned Italian-*
　style tomatoes
1½ *cups beef broth*
¾ *cup chopped*
　mushrooms
1½ *teaspoons salt*
½ *teaspoon freshly ground*
　black pepper

Toss the beef with the flour. Heat the oil in a saucepan; sauté the onions, carrots, and parsley 10 minutes. Add the beef; cook until no red remains, stirring frequently to prevent lumps from forming. Add the wine; cook over high heat 3 minutes. Mix in the tomatoes, broth, mushrooms, salt, and pepper. Cook over low heat 1½ hours. Taste for seasoning. Serve with any *pasta*.

Makes about 3 cups.

BOLOGNESE SAUCE I
(Ragu)

2 *tablespoons butter*
¼ *pound ham, cut julienne*
¾ *cup chopped onions*
¼ *cup chopped celery*
½ *cup grated carrots*
¾ *pound ground beef*
½ *pound chicken livers,*
　diced

1½ *tablespoons tomato*
　paste
¾ *cup dry white wine*
1½ *cups water*
1 *teaspoon salt*
½ *teaspoon freshly ground*
　black pepper
⅛ *teaspoon nutmeg*

Melt the butter in a saucepan; sauté the ham, onions, celery, and carrots 10 minutes, stirring frequently. Add the beef; cook over medium heat, stirring almost constantly, until browned. Add the livers and cook 2 minutes, stirring constantly. Blend in the tomato paste, then stir in the wine, water, salt, pepper, and nutmeg. Cover and cook over low heat 45 minutes, stirring frequently. Taste for seasoning. For a richer sauce, add 1 cup heavy cream before mixing with the *pasta*. Serve with all *pasta*.

Makes about 3 cups.

BOLOGNESE SAUCE II

6 *tablespoons butter*
1 *cup finely chopped*
   onions
½ *cup grated carrots*
1 *pound ground beef*
1 *8-ounce can tomato sauce*

4 *cups beef broth or water*
1½ *teaspoons salt*
½ *teaspoon freshly ground*
   black pepper
1 *cup heavy cream*

Melt the butter in a saucepan; sauté the onions and carrots 10 minutes. Add the beef; cook, stirring frequently, until no pink remains. Add the tomato sauce, broth, salt, and pepper; cover and cook over low heat 2 hours, stirring occasionally. Mix in the cream and taste for seasoning.

Makes about 5 cups.

ITALIAN MIXED MEAT SAUCE

¼ *pound salt pork, diced*
¾ *cup chopped onions*
½ *cup sliced carrots*
1 *pound ground beef*
¼ *pound ground veal*
¼ *pound ground pork*
1½ *cups beef broth*
1¼ *teaspoons salt*

½ *teaspoon freshly ground*
   black pepper
3 *cups boiling water*
1 *teaspoon tomato paste*
¼ *pound mushrooms,*
   chopped
½ *cup heavy cream*

Lightly brown the salt pork in a saucepan. Pour off half the fat. Add the onions and carrots; sauté 5 minutes. Add the beef, veal, and pork; cook over medium heat 5 minutes, stirring almost constantly. Mix in the broth; cook over low heat 15 minutes. Add the salt, pepper, water, and tomato paste; cover and cook over low heat 1 hour. Mix in the mushrooms; cook 15 minutes longer. Blend in the cream and taste for seasoning. Serve on spaghetti or noodles.

Makes about 3½ cups.

WHITE SAUCE

(Béchamel Sauce)

3 cups milk	*⅓ cup flour*
3 tablespoons minced onion	*½ teaspoon salt*
1 bay leaf	*Dash white pepper*
4 tablespoons butter	

Bring the milk (or milk and stock), onion and bay leaf to a boil. Let stand 15 minutes and strain.

Melt the butter in a saucepan; blend in the flour, until flour turns golden. Gradually add the strained liquid stirring constantly to the boiling point. Stir in the salt and pepper. Cook over low heat 20 minutes, stirring frequently; strain.

Makes about 2 cups.

Desexts

*D*ESSERTS are a delightful conclusion for any meal, and an imaginative dessert makes a lasting impression. *Pasta* provides a novel change from the ever-present pie or cake, and desserts containing *pasta* are much easier to prepare. A word of caution: Don't serve any of the desserts in this section if the preceding dishes were heavy or contained another starch. Instead, save the novel desserts as the satisfying complement to a light meal.

NOODLE DESSERT SOUFFLE

3 egg yolks	½ pound medium noodles,
3 tablespoons sugar	cooked and drained
½ cup melted butter	4 egg whites
2 cups cottage cheese	¼ cup ground almonds
1 cup sour cream	3 tablespoons butter

Beat the egg yolks and sugar until thick. Stir in the melted butter, then the cheese and sour cream until smooth. Fold in the noodles.

Beat the egg whites until stiff but not dry; fold into the noodle mixture. Turn into a 2-quart buttered soufflé dish or casserole. Sprinkle with the nuts and dot with the butter. Bake in a preheated 375° oven 45 minutes.

Serves 6–8.

FRENCH NOODLE PUDDING
(Pouding de Nouilles)

3½ cups milk	¼ pound butter
½ pound fine noodles	5 egg yolks
½ cup sugar	4 egg whites
⅛ teaspoon salt	¼ cup bread crumbs

Bring the milk to a boil in a saucepan. Gradually add the noodles, stirring constantly. Mix in the sugar, salt, and all but 1 tablespoon of the butter. Cook over low heat 20 minutes.

Beat the egg yolks in a bowl. Gradually add noodle mixture, mixing steadily to prevent curdling. Cool 10 minutes. Beat the egg whites until stiff but not dry. Fold into the noodle mixture. Butter a baking dish with the remaining butter and dust with the bread crumbs. Pour the noodle mixture into it.

Place dish in a pan. Add enough hot water to reach halfway up the dish. Bake in a 350° oven 30 minutes, or until pudding is firm to the touch. Serve hot or cold.

Serves 6–8.

BAKED APPLE AND NOODLE CASSEROLE

6 apples, peeled, cored, and sliced	¼ cup melted butter
	¼ pound cream cheese
¼ cup firmly packed brown sugar	¼ cup light cream
	¾ pound fine noodles, cooked and drained
1 teaspoon cinnamon	
½ teaspoon salt	

Combine the apples, brown sugar, cinnamon, salt, and butter in a bowl. Toss lightly. Mash cream cheese with the cream and toss with the noodles. Mix in the apple mixture. Pour into a buttered

2-quart casserole. Bake in a 350° oven 40 minutes. Serve hot or cold.
Serves 6–8.

LAYERED DESSERT NOODLE PUDDING

3 eggs
¼ cup sugar
¼ teaspoon salt
1 teaspoon cinnamon
½ pound broad noodles,
    cooked and drained

⅓ cup melted butter
½ cup chopped seedless
    raisins or candied fruit
¼ cup chopped nuts
3 tablespoons cake or
    cooky crumbs

Beat the eggs in a bowl, then beat in the sugar, salt, and cinnamon. Fold in the noodles and melted butter.

Pour half the mixture into a buttered baking dish. Spread the raisins and nuts over it. Cover with the remaining noodles. Sprinkle with the crumbs. Bake in a 375° oven 40 minutes, or until the mixture is set and browned on top. Serve hot or cold.
Serves 4–6.

ITALIAN FETTUCCINE PUDDING

(Budino di Pasta)

1 pound fettuccine,
    cooked and drained
4 eggs
1½ cups sugar

4 cups milk
1 teaspoon vanilla extract
2 teaspoons cinnamon
½ teaspoon nutmeg

Spread the *fettuccine* in a buttered baking dish.

Beat the eggs, gradually adding the sugar. Beat in the milk, vanilla, and cinnamon. Pour over the *fettuccine*. Sprinkle with the nutmeg.

Bake in a preheated 350° oven 20 minutes, or until set. Chill.
Serves 8–10.

MALAYAN DESSERT

4 *tablespoons butter*	½ *pound vermicelli*
½ *cup cashew nuts*	2 *cups milk*
4 *tablespoons seedless*	1¼ *cups sugar*
raisins	1 *teaspoon vanilla extract*

Melt half the butter in a saucepan. Sauté the nuts and raisins 5 minutes, then remove from the pan. Melt the remaining butter in the same saucepan; sauté the vermicelli, stirring constantly, 5 minutes. Add the milk. Bring to a boil and cook over low heat 10 minutes.

Add the sugar and cook 5 minutes, stirring occasionally. Remove from the heat. Add the vanilla, nuts, and raisins and stir together. Serve hot.

Serves 4–6.

TURKISH NOODLE DESSERT

(Kataiyiff)

1 *pound fine noodles,*	1¼ *cups honey*
cooked and drained	3 *tablespoons butter*
1 *cup coarsely chopped*	
almonds	

Place the noodles in a well-buttered baking dish. Chill until firm. Sprinkle the almonds and then the honey on top. Dot with the butter.

Bake in a 350° oven 25 minutes. Cut into squares and serve hot or cold.

Serves 8–10.

ANGLO-INDIAN FESTIVAL DESSERT

(Savia)

¼ pound (1 stick) butter
1 pound vermicelli,
    broken in half
½ teaspoon salt
Boiling water
¼ cup seedless raisins

¼ cup pistachio nuts
¼ cup slivered blanched
    almonds
1 cup finely grated coconut
¼ cup confectioners' sugar
1 cup heavy cream

Melt the butter in a saucepan. Add the vermicelli. Cook over low heat 5 minutes, stirring almost constantly. Add the salt and boiling water barely to cover. Cover and cook over low heat until the water is absorbed and the vermicelli tender. Mix occasionally with 2 forks. Mix in the raisins, pistachios, and almonds lightly. Heap on a platter and sprinkle with the coconut and sugar. Serve with the cream, either plain or whipped.

Serves 4–6.

INDIAN VERMICELLI DESSERT

3 tablespoons honey
3 tablespoons sugar
1 cup water
1¾ cups vermicelli

6 tablespoons butter
¼ cup slivered blanched
    almonds
¼ teaspoon nutmeg

Combine the honey, sugar, and water in a saucepan; bring to a boil and cook over high heat 4 minutes. While the syrup is cooking, break the vermicelli into small pieces. Melt the butter in a skillet; add the vermicelli and cook, stirring almost steadily, until browned. Mix in the almonds. Add the syrup, mixing well. Cook until syrup is absorbed. Mix in the nutmeg. Serve hot.

Serves 4–6.

SWEET NOODLE DESSERT

3 cups milk
1 cup light cream
½ teaspoon salt
5 tablespoons butter
½ cup granulated sugar
½ cup uncooked fine
   noodles

¼ cup currants or seedless
   raisins
1 teaspoon vanilla extract
2 tablespoons dry bread
   crumbs

Combine the milk, cream, salt, 4 tablespoons of the butter, and ⅓ cup of the sugar in a saucepan. Bring to a boil. Add the noodles. Cook over medium heat 10 minutes, or until the noodles are almost tender and the liquid is absorbed, stirring frequently. Mix in the currants and vanilla.

Butter an 8-inch-square baking pan with the remaining butter. Dust with the bread crumbs. Pour the noodle mixture into it. Bake in a 425° oven 20 minutes, or until browned and crisp on top. Turn out carefully onto a serving dish and dust with the remaining sugar.

Serves 4–6.

NOODLES AND HONEY

(Strufuli)

2 cups sifted flour
½ teaspoon salt
3 eggs, beaten

Vegetable oil for deep-fat
   frying
1 cup honey
½ cup chopped nuts

Sift the flour and salt onto a board. Make a well in the center and place the eggs in it. Work in the flour until a dough is formed. Knead very well. If dough is too soft, add a little flour and knead again. Break off a piece of the dough and roll between lightly floured hands into long pieces, about ½ inch in circumference. Cut into ½-inch lengths.

Heat the oil to 380°. Drop the pieces into the oil, a few at a time. Fry until delicately browned. Drain well. Place them in a deep bowl.

Heat the honey and pour over the fried noodles. Stir gently. Add the nuts gradually as you stir. Form several small mounds of the mixture. Cool.

Serves 6–8.

MACARONI IN MILK

(Maccheroni con Latte)

½ *pound macaroni*	¼ *cups sugar*
4 *cups milk*	1 *teaspoon cinnamon*

Cook the macaroni 2 minutes less than package directs. Drain. Return to saucepan; add the milk. Bring to a boil and cook over low heat 5 minutes, stirring frequently. Mix in the sugar and cinnamon.

Serves 4.

CHEESE-RAISIN PUDDING

4 *eggs*	1 *pound fine noodles,*
¾ *cup sour cream*	*cooked and drained*
¼ *cup sugar*	4 *tablespoons dry bread*
1 *teaspoon salt*	*crumbs*
2 *cups cottage cheese*	3 *tablespoons melted butter*
½ *cup seedless raisins*	

Beat the eggs, sour cream, sugar, and salt together. Stir in the cheese, raisins, and noodles. Turn into a buttered 2-quart baking dish or casserole. Sprinkle with the bread crumbs and butter. Bake in a 375° oven 40 minutes.

Serves 6.

NOODLE-PRUNE PUDDING

1 cup orange juice	½ cup seedless raisins
½ pound prunes	1 pound fine noodles,
2 eggs	cooked and drained
¼ cup sugar	3 tablespoons melted
¼ teaspoon salt	butter
½ teaspoon cinnamon	

Bring the orange juice and prunes to a boil; let soak 1 hour. Drain. Remove the pits and chop the prunes.

Beat the eggs, sugar, salt, and cinnamon together. Stir in the prunes, raisins, noodles, and melted butter. Turn into a greased 1½-quart baking dish. Bake in a 400° oven 30 minutes, or until browned.

Serves 6–8.

BANANA-NOODLE DESSERT

4 tablespoons butter	1 egg yolk
1 tablespoon flour	1 cup heavy cream, scalded
½ teaspoon salt	2 bananas, finely mashed
½ cup light cream	½ pound medium noodles,
½ cup milk	cooked and drained
½ cup sugar	

Melt the butter in a saucepan. Blend in the flour and salt. Add the light cream and milk, stirring constantly to the boiling point. Add the sugar. Cook over low heat 3 minutes, stirring frequently.

Beat the egg yolk in a bowl. Gradually add the hot mixture, stirring constantly to prevent curdling. Return to saucepan. Cook over very low heat 2 minutes, stirring constantly. Remove from heat. Mix the heavy cream with the mashed bananas. Slowly add to the hot mixture, stirring constantly.

Divide the noodles among 6 individual dishes and pour the sauce over them.

Serves 6.

APPLE-NOODLE PUDDING

½ cup currants or seedless
    raisins
¼ cup sherry
4 tablespoons butter
4 apples, peeled and sliced
3 egg yolks

¾ cup sugar
¼ teaspoon salt
1 teaspoon cinnamon
¼ pound medium noodles,
    cooked and drained
3 egg whites

Soak the currants in the sherry 15 minutes. Drain.

Melt the butter in a skillet; sauté the apples 5 minutes. Beat the egg yolks in a bowl; then beat in the sugar, salt, and cinnamon. Mix in the currants, noodles, and apples. Beat the egg whites until stiff but not dry. Fold into the previous mixture carefully. Pour into a 1½-quart buttered baking dish.

Bake in a 375° oven 30 minutes. Serve hot with heavy sweet cream. If desired, the pudding may be served cold with whipped cream.

Serves 4–6.

SWEET GNOCCHI

3 eggs
2 tablespoons sugar
1 cup sifted flour
1 cup milk
3 tablespoons butter
2 egg yolks

1 tablespoon grated orange
   rind
¼ cup sifted confectioners'
   sugar
1 teaspoon cinnamon
¼ cup cooky crumbs

Beat the eggs lightly in the top of a double boiler. Mix in the sugar and flour. Gradually add the milk, stirring steadily, then add butter. Place over hot water and cook, stirring constantly, until smooth and thick, about 10 minutes.

Beat the egg yolks in a bowl. Gradually add the hot mixture, stirring constantly to prevent curdling. Add the orange rind. Pour mixture onto a well-floured surface. Cool 20 minutes. Shape into 1-inch balls. Carefully drop into boiling water. Cook 5 minutes, or until the *gnocchi* float. Drain well.

Arrange the *gnocchi* in layers on a serving dish. Sprinkle with the sugar, cinnamon, and crumbs. Serve hot.

Serves 4–6.

SWEET RAVIOLI

(Ravioli Dolci)

2 cups sifted flour
¼ teaspoon salt
2 eggs, beaten
2 teaspoons lukewarm
   water
½ pound ricotta cheese or
   cottage cheese

¼ cup confectioners' sugar
¼ cup candied fruit,
   chopped
1 egg yolk, beaten
1 teaspoon vanilla extract
Vegetable oil for deep-fat
   frying

Sift the flour and salt together onto a board. Make a well in the center and place the eggs and water in it. Work in the flour until a dough is formed. Knead until smooth and elastic. Cover and set aside 20 minutes. Roll out the dough ¼ inch thick. Cut into 3-inch circles.

Beat together the ricotta cheese, confectioners' sugar, candied fruit, egg yolk, and vanilla until fluffy. Place a heaping teaspoonful of the mixture on each circle of dough. Fold over the dough, sealing the edges well with a little egg white or water.

Heat the oil to 370°. Fry a few *ravioli* at a time until delicately brown. Drain well. Serve hot with confectioners' sugar, if desired. *Serves 8–10.*

FRIED DESSERT NOODLES

2 cups sifted flour
½ teaspoon salt
⅓ cup sugar
6 eggs
¾ cup light cream

¾ cup sweet sherry
Vegetable oil for deep-fat
   frying
¼ cup confectioners' sugar

Sift the flour, salt, and sugar into a bowl. Beat the eggs; add the cream and sherry. Add to the flour mixture, beating until very smooth.

Heat the oil to 370°. Pour the batter through a funnel into the fat in short lengths. Do not fry too many at one time. Fry until very lightly browned. Drain. Sprinkle with the confectioners' sugar. Serve hot or cold. *Serves 4–6.*

MACARONI WITH WHIPPED CREAM

¼ pound butter
3 tablespoons grated
   Parmesan cheese
2 cups ground almonds

1 pound elbow macaroni,
   cooked and drained
2 cups whipped cream

Melt the butter in a saucepan. Add the cheese, almonds, and macaroni. Toss over low heat 2 minutes. Fold in the whipped cream and turn into a baking dish. Place under the broiler until delicately browned. Serve immediately.

Serves 4–6.

SOUR-CREAM NOODLES

4 tablespoons butter
¼ cup poppy seeds
½ cup blanched, sliced
    almonds

1 teaspoon salt
½ pound broad noodles,
    cooked and drained
1 cup sour cream

Melt the butter in a saucepan. Add the poppy seeds, almonds, and salt, mixing together lightly. Add the noodles, tossing lightly. Mix in the sour cream gently. Cook over low heat 5 minutes.

Serves 2–4.

NOODLES WITH POPPY SEEDS

½ pound poppy seeds,
    ground
1 cup milk
½ cup honey
½ cup heavy cream
1 teaspoon grated lemon
    rind
⅛ teaspoon salt

1 teaspoon vanilla extract
¼ cup coarsely chopped
    almonds
1 pound medium noodles,
    cooked and drained
4 tablespoons melted
    butter

If possible, have the poppy seeds ground at the store where they are purchased. If not, grind them in a mortar or blender.

Soak the poppy seeds in the milk 2 hours. Drain.

Combine the honey, cream, lemon rind, salt, and poppy seeds in a saucepan. Cook over low heat, stirring frequently, until the mixture is thick. Stir in the vanilla and almonds.

Toss the noodles with the melted butter. Put the noodles on a platter and pour the poppy-seed mixture over them; toss lightly.

Serves 4–6.

PASTINA WITH BUTTER AND NUTS

(Pastina con Buro e Noci)

¼ *pound butter*
1 *cup ground almonds or*
    walnuts

1 *teaspoon salt*
1 *pound pastina, cooked*
    and drained

Melt the butter in a skillet but do not allow it to brown. Add the nuts and salt. Cook over very low heat 3 minutes, stirring almost constantly.

Place the pastina in a serving dish. Pour the butter-nut mixture over it and toss lightly.

Serves 4–6.

CARAMEL-ALMOND NOODLES

1¼ *cups brown sugar*
½ *cup granulated sugar*
⅓ *cup heavy cream*
6 *tablespoons butter*

½ *cup blanched, sliced*
    almonds
½ *pound fine noodles,*
    cooked and drained

Combine the brown sugar, granulated sugar, cream, and butter in a saucepan. Cook over low heat until sugar is dissolved and mixture begins to thicken, about 5 minutes. Mix in the almonds and noodles lightly but thoroughly. Pour into a buttered 8-inch-square baking dish. Bake in a 425° oven 10 minutes. Serve hot or cold.

Serves 4–6.

NOODLES WITH HAZELNUTS

¼ *pound sweet butter*
½ *cup sugar*
1 *cup chopped hazelnuts*
    (filberts)

1 *pound broad noodles,*
    cooked and drained

Cream the butter. Gradually add the sugar and nuts, beating until well blended. Add the hot noodles and toss lightly until well coated with the mixture. Serve immediately.

Serves 4–6.

FRIED BOWKNOTS

(Farfallette)

1½ *cups sifted flour*
1 *tablespoon butter*
3 *eggs*
⅛ *teaspoon salt*
2 *tablespoons sugar*

½ *teaspoon orange extract*
Vegetable oil for deep-fat
    frying
Confectioners' sugar

Sift the flour into a bowl; work in the butter. Beat together the eggs, salt, sugar, and orange extract. Stir into the flour mixture. Knead on a lightly floured surface until smooth; if too soft, add a little flour. Cover and set aside for 30 minutes. Break off pieces of dough and roll as thin as possible. Cut into strips ¾-inch wide by 5 inches long; tie into bowknots.

Heat the oil to 375° and fry a few at a time until browned. Drain and sprinkle with confectioners' sugar.

Makes about 48.

A PARTIAL LIST OF MACARONI SHAPES

(There are over 150 different shapes in the United States, not all available in all areas.)

elbow macaroni

long macaroni

shells

jumbo shells

lasagne

curly lasagne

mafalde

ziti

mezzani

mezzani rigati

mostaccioli

mostaccioli rigati

rigatoni

tufoli

ditali

ditalini

manicotti

manicotti rigati

alphabets

pastina

creste di gallo

riccini

gnocchi

cantelli

margherite

occhi di lupo

cavatelli

rotelli

rotini

tubettini

maccaroncelli

fettuccelle

spaghetti

spaghettini

vermicelli

cut spaghetti

linguini

fusilli

folded egg noodles

   fine

   medium

   wide

egg noodles (not folded)

   fine

   medium

   wide

egg noodles

   extra fine

   broad

egg barley

egg flakes

egg wheels

spinach egg noodles

bows or butterflies

   small

   large

egg rings

fancy egg rings

rosa marina

stellini

kluski

bott boi

haluska

Index

Creste di Gallo

Folded Fine Egg Noodles

Wide Egg Noodles

Folded Medium Egg Noodles

Cavatelli

Mafalde

Curly-Edged Lasagne

Manicotti Rigati

Mostaccioli

Medium Egg Noodles

Long Macaroni

Maccaroncelli

Margherite